WHAT I AM PLEASED TO CALL
MY EDUCATION

WHAT I AM PLEASED TO CALL MY EDUCATION

BY HENRY WATSON KENT

EDITED BY LOIS LEIGHTON COMINGS

THE GROLIER CLUB · NEW YORK

1949

PREFACE

I CONFESS TO HAVE been flattered by the request to write
my memoirs, which now cover a long lifetime — and the
more flattered as the request came from my long-time friend
and associate in the Secretary's office of the Metropolitan
Museum, Lauder Greenway, who must have been tired to
death already by hearing me reminisce about things of the
past, at a time when he couldn't escape. There is nothing
remarkable to chronicle, unless it was noteworthy to have
grown up at a time when something always seemed to be
happening in the world that interested me most, the public
museum world. A sickly boy, I was denied the early training
in school and college which I should have had, but I can't
help thinking that the education I got by my own incentive,
following my own bent, was as wide as most boys get in college. So I have set down the things that helped me to do
what I did, sometimes trivial things, you may think, but
they, like the traditional many mickles, made my muckle.

When I went to the Metropolitan Museum, I was not conscious of having learned much of use to me there. But now,
in writing these things about Norwich and The Grolier
Club, I can see I had real teachers, in Norwich itself, in
Daniel Coit Gilman, Charles Eliot Norton, Theodore De
Vinne, and The Grolier Club, and, going back still further,
in Melvil Dewey.

I have not tried to write a history, though I may, by
chance, have added something to the Slater Museum's pub-

lished record. The history of the Metropolitan Museum has been admirably done by Miss Winifred E. Howe in two volumes, and no one could do it better. What I have attempted to tell of are the things seen and heard in my life, and what they did for me in fitting me for work in museums. I have a notion that it may be these perceptions, not counted as educational at the moment they are experienced, which serve us best in life.

I am grateful to all those good friends who have encouraged me in writing these memoirs, to Miss Lois Leighton Comings, without whose help they could not have been written, and to Miss Winifred E. Howe, who read the book in manuscript, bringing to it her personal knowledge of Norwich and the Metropolitan Museum, and her long editorial experience. I am grateful to all those kind, friendly helpers of the past who made the work wherever done possible, and who helped to give it whatever success it may have had.

H. W. KENT

June 23, 1948

vi

TABLE OF CONTENTS

LIST OF ILLUSTRATIONS

INTRODUCTION

As THE TWIG is bent, the tree is inclined. Henry Kent never forgot the lessons learned as a young assistant at the Boston Public Library, or as a student in the first Columbia Library School class under Melvil Dewey; he never forgot what he learned as the first Curator and the Librarian at the Slater Museum and Peck Library of Norwich Free Academy, or among the American antiques of Norwichtown; he never forgot what he learned among the museums abroad under the early influence of Wilhelm Bode; he never forgot what he learned as the first professional Librarian of The Grolier Club.

An interest in books on art led him to help in the building up of the Metropolitan Museum's superb library. An interest in exactitude of method led to the well-drilled organization of all the departments of that museum which were under his oversight. An interest in the interpretation of collections to the public and to industry, first exercised at Norwich, led to his pioneering in those regards in New York. An interest in Americana led to the American section of the Hudson-Fulton exhibition and to the American Wing of the Metropolitan. An interest in the technique of museum display and organization led to his association in the founding of the national body of the profession, the American Association of Museums.

It is a sign one has built well when the institutions one has helped to found or to build continue long to survive and grow. Just today I have a card from the Slater Memorial Museum announcing an exhibition of contemporary textiles by leading designers and manufacturers. Next month the American Association of Museums, with a membership now numbering institutions by the hundred, individuals by the thousand, holds its forty-second annual meeting. The Walpole Society, at once convivial and serious, continues to flourish as the inner circle of collectors and connoisseurs of early American art. The Grolier Club stoutly maintains its position and its ancient ideals.

Behind his cool reserve, Henry Kent has always had a warm heart. His friendships have been wide and deep; his generosity and help to young men, notable. To speak personally, I shall never forget that it was he who, when I was but thirty, risked asking me to give the series of lectures at the Metropolitan which preceded the building of the American Wing, and which resulted in my book, *The Domestic Architecture of the American Colonies,* published for the Museum. It was he, too, soon afterwards, who sent to see me, at a distant university, William Sloane Coffin, later President of the Museum—a visit which led to my being called to New York to found what is now the Institute of Fine Arts of New York University, and thus ultimately to the post I now hold. I am sure there must have been, concealed by his modesty, many other instances of the sort.

There were numerous ways in which the author could have written his memories. One he did not adopt was the "now it can be told" method — revealing the "anxieties, ingenuities, and machinations," as he says once in passing. Miss Howe's two-volume history of the Metropolitan is necessarily so official that many would have welcomed an inside story of the Museum, with its "lordly curators," its schisms, its scandals, and its controversies. Some of the personalities involved are still living; it was no doubt a consideration for them as well as his own natural reticence which led him to pass over these in silence.

His closing quotation from Professor Whitehead characterizes not only his subject matter but himself, when it speaks of "the most austere of all mental qualities, a sense of style," and, as fundamental aesthetic qualities, of "attainment and restraint."

FISKE KIMBALL

Philadelphia Museum of Art
April, 1948

WHAT I AM PLEASED TO CALL
MY EDUCATION

CHAPTER I

NORWICH

SCHOOLDAYS

I AM OF YANKEE STOCK, all of my forebears having come to Massachusetts in its beginning, and I was brought up on stories of these ancestors, their ways and manners—Watsons and Winslows of Plymouth, Hobarts of Hingham, and Kents of Kent's Island, Newburyport. Puritans, Pilgrims, Indians, and royal governors were all subjects of the talk I heard in my early days. My father was a good storyteller and singer of early Yankee songs, like "Captain Jinks of the Horse Marines," who had inherited his gift for this sort of thing from his father. My maternal great-grandfather had thirty ships plying between Boston and China, my grandfather was a captain in the War of 1812, and some of my Kents were at Bunker Hill. So, you see, I was started out in life in true New England fashion, with a love of the past and enough of the characteristics of Puritanism in me to make life miserable or interesting, according to circumstances.

I was born in Boston, and went to the Latin School for a time, but eventually I was put to school in the 1

Free Academy of Norwich, Connecticut; this was in
1881.

Norwich had been one of the most influential towns
of the state in Colonial and Revolutionary times, and
after the Civil War it became an important manufacturing city, but the old part of the town, Norwichtown,
as it is now called, kept its Colonial character, in houses,
people, manners, and customs. The houses around the
old green (green is the Connecticut name for what in
Massachusetts is called a common), originally of the
seventeenth century, had gradually been renovated to
suit the later fashions in dwellings, but many of them
had kept their original woodwork, paneling and shut-
ters, and chimneys. Everything about the place recalled
the old times, and to a boy from the city who was naturally impressed by such things, it was a delight.

The Norwich Free Academy, of which I shall have
more to say in later chapters, had just concluded its first
twenty-five years of existence, and was then a well-estab-
lished secondary school of excellent repute. It was not
a boarding school, however, and therefore my sister
and I were given into the care of the Reverend Charles
T. Weitzel, minister of the old first Congregational
Church, and his wife, Sophy Winthrop Weitzel. These
arrangements were made for us as the result of a suggestion to my older brother by Mr. William Gilman,
brother of President Daniel Coit Gilman of Johns Hopkins, and with the friendly help of his three sisters,
then living in Norwichtown in the old Lathrop house,
where Lydia Huntley Sigourney lived during her early
childhood.

2

This was a piece of rare good fortune for me. While for the next three years my education at the Academy went on in the usual way, without special occurrences except that I won a prize in drawing, in the Parsonage I was receiving most skillful and tender guidance. Mr. Weitzel had been born in Germany, and with him I began the study of German. He was the eighth pastor of the two hundred and twenty-two year old church and preached in its fifth meetinghouse, which faced the green; from him I heard much of the Puritans and their oligarchy, and the origin of the Congregational Church in Connecticut. His wife, I believe, taught me more than any professional teacher I ever had. She wrote verses, articles for the *Spectator* and the *Outlook,* and books for young people, including two in the "No Name" series published by Roberts. Books and music for her were a natural part of life; she was cultured without affectation. Under her tutelage, as we read together in her quiet parlor, Milton's poems and *The Pilgrim's Progress* became mine, Ruskin, Carlyle, and other English authors were explained to me, and my taste in such matters and in music was gently trained. Mrs. Weitzel helped me to acquire a love of the book itself, also, as well as of literature, an interest which, later, was to serve me in good stead.

Because of Mrs. Weitzel's health, the Weitzels left Norwichtown for California in 1885. Until the last weeks before her death in 1892 her letters were frequent, following my doings with understanding and wise counsel.

Mrs. Weitzel's sister was the wife of William Hutch-

ison, affectionately called "Tutor Hutchison," principal of the Academy from 1865 to 1885. He was
particularly interested in botany, and we were all
given courses in botany, using Gray's *How Plants
Grow*. At this time, all Norwich of a certain age went
botanizing in the spring, and they still keep it up,
young and old.

My room at the Weitzels' was the parlor of the
typical old eighteenth-century house, unusually well
paneled, painted blue, before white paint came into
fashion. One day a visiting clergyman, old Father
Shipman, they called him, coming to preach the Sunday sermon, at his request was given my room, so that
he could easily find his way across the street to Parson
Arms's privy if necessary, which he said he knew better
how to use than newfangled devices. Parson Arms, by
the way, had been the Pastor and Pastor Emeritus of
this old meetinghouse for nearly fifty years, and one
of the Trustees of Yale College for the same length of
time. Arrangements were made for me to sleep the
night of Father Shipman's visit at the big Ebenezer
Huntington House, called "Huntington's Folly," the
most elegant and aristocratic house, at this time the
home of the "Ladies Huntington." These were four
daughters of General Ebenezer Huntington, son of
Major General Jabez, an important figure in the Revolution. There lived with them a niece, Miss Sarah
Perkins, who, like her aunts, retained the hoopskirt all
her life, and I must admit to you that after I went to
New York I used to buy them for her, down on Sixth
Avenue. She wore a ring on her index finger composed

of a great cluster of diamonds, and her passion was the study of Egyptian history. I owed my introduction to the work of the English Egypt Exploration Society to the fact that she subscribed to its publications, and lent them to me.

Ebenezer was one of five sons, four of whom were active, like their father, in the Revolution, the fifth being too young to serve. Ebenezer left Yale College in April, 1775, to join the army, and his letters to his father during his service from the beginning to the end of the war were carefully kept by his daughters. Later, I had them copied and I asked Professor Edward Bourne of Yale to edit them. He did, and they were published in the *American Historical Review* of July, 1900.

The Ladies Huntington are so well described in a poem by Edmund Clarence Stedman, the "banker poet," that I will quote it. He himself was a Norwich personage and destined to become my friend.

HUNTINGTON HOUSE[1]

Ladies, Ladies Huntington, your father served, we
    know,
As aide-de-camp to Washington — you often told
    us so;
And when you sat you side by side in that ancestral
    pew,
We knew his ghost sat next the door, and very proud
    of you.

Ladies, Ladies Huntington, like you there are no
    more:
Nancy, Sarah, Emily, Louise, — proud maidens four;

5

Nancy tall and angular, Louise a rosy dear,
And Emily as fine as lace but just a little sere.

What was it, pray, your life within the mansion grand
    and old,
Four dormers in its gambrel-roof, their shingles grim
    with mould?
How dwelt you in your spinsterhood, ye ancient
    virgins lone,
From infancy to bag-and-muff so resolutely grown?

Each Sunday morning out you drove to Parson Arms's
    church,
As straight as if Time had not left you somehow in
    the lurch;
And so lived where your grandfather and father lived
    and died,
Until you sought them one by one — and last of all
    stayed pride.

You knew that with them you would lie in that old
    burial ground
Wherethrough the name of Huntington on vault
    and stone is found,
Where Norwichtown's first infant male, in sixteen-
    sixty born,
Grave Christopher, still rests beneath his cherub
    carved forlorn.

There sleep your warlike ancestors, their feet toward
    the east,
And thus shall face the Judgment Throne when
    Gabriel's blast hath ceased.
The frost of years may heave the tomb whereto you
    were consigned,
And school-boys peer atween the cracks, but you —
    will never mind.

6

The ladies received me in the parlor, wearing hoop-skirts, cuffs and collars, and cameo pins, like the *Godey's Lady's Book* pictures of the Victorian period, and, to amuse me, they showed me the treasures that were kept in the splendid block-front mahogany desk which Washington himself had used at Cambridge and which fortunately is now in the American Wing. Here were fans, slippers, and caps worn by the ladies when they danced with Lafayette and other notables in the hall of the house, during the Frenchman's visit to their father, and many other mementoes of distinguished occasions. Lafayette, by the way, came three times to Norwich, once, Miss Caulkins[2] says, with no stockings on! Washington came in June, 1775, on his way to Cambridge, and the next year in April, after the evacuation of Boston by the British, he came again and met Governor Jonathan Trumbull at the house of Colonel Jedediah Huntington (another son of Jabez), where they dined together. The Duke de Lauzun came also, with his hussars. All of these things the ladies talked about, you may be sure.

When bedtime came, I was asked to pull the bell rope, and the bell was answered by a colored woman, a descendant of a slave of the family. (The Norwichtown graveyard has a whole corner filled with the graves of slaves, and on each side of the lane leading into it were buried some twenty French soldiers who, in 1778, died in Norwich of a fever.) She, being told to show me to my room, led me out into the central hall, where upon a table full of candles in silver candlesticks we found two for my use. These she lit, and then, going before, she led me up the beautiful staircase, which ascended in three runs with a square landing at each turn, with a fine newel and balusters, to a room with four windows. The bed where I was to sleep was a four-poster, with tester and valance and sheets redolent of lavender.

Here was an experience, a whiff of the past for a young Boston boy, never to be forgotten! A reasonable thought, which such a boy might have engendered in him in going from Boston into Connecticut, was about the narrow-mindedness of Massachusetts people, who knew nothing of Connecticut men and things. As I learned later, the minute you cross the line from Massachusetts into Connecticut you are in a different country.

NOTES

[1] Dated 1894. *The Poems of Edmund Clarence Stedman*, Boston: Houghton Mifflin Company, 1908, pp. 130-131.

[2] Norwich's historian. See below, pp. 75-76 and p. 85, n. 1.

LIBRARY TRAINING IN BOSTON AND COLUMBIA

READING, AS I HAVE done recently in the *Museum News*, the articles by various directors of museums on the kind of training they thought was required for curators and such like people in art museums, I am led to think of the training which I received, as one of the first among those who adopted the new "profession of museum worker," as we delighted to call it. There were no schools to teach us who were interested in such training in those days, when this "profession" was not recognized, by colleges or anybody else. There were no books or magazines devoted to this interest for us to read. If we were in earnest, we had to depend upon ourselves to get whatever we thought would make us desired and useful.

At the risk of seeming very conceited, or self-satisfied, or what you like, I am inclined to tell of my education for such work, even if sometimes I may be stretching a point to fit my case. Education, after all, is the grist one's mill grinds out. However good, bad, or insignificant it may be, it becomes one's stock in trade.

I, fortunately for me, after trying in vain to get a   9

job in a publishing house, in the summer of 1884 went to work to earn my living in the Boston Public Library, in the "well-designed" old building down on Boylston Street, built in 1858 by C. F. Kirby. Here I was taught to open books, count signatures, and, generally, do boy's work, under the direction of a devoted and exacting taskmaster, Miss Fuller, the niece of Margaret Fuller, the Countess Ossoli, of Brook Farm.

No mistake or slipshod work was allowed by Miss Fuller — any fault in the pagination of a book required that it be returned to its publisher, but any carelessness in cutting the leaves of a book or in opening a stiffly bound volume was reprimanded by raps with a ruler over the knuckles. All employees of the Library in those days, from the top to the bottom, were required to change their shoes for slippers on entering the building in the morning, and their coats for "dusters," as they were called. All of this routine was good discipline, teaching quietness and consideration for others — excellent training for public servants.

While I was in the Public Library, I heard of a training school for people who wanted to work in libraries professionally, to become librarians. I received the notice one day, printed in light blue ink, which told of the opportunity for those who desired to embrace the "profession of librarianship" (a fine expression) to receive instruction in Library Economy (grand and unusual words) in the Library of Columbia College. This notice was signed by Melvil Dewey, who had come from Amherst College, where he had been its

Assistant Librarian, to Columbia in 1883, upon the completion of its new library building on Forty-ninth Street, off Madison Avenue. Desiring now to embrace this profession, to Columbia I went, fearfully, in the autumn of 1884, as a member of this first group of young men and women whose study and practical work in the Columbia College Library were preliminary to the official opening of the School of Library Economy in January, 1887.[1]

The Library building, shared with the Law School, delighted me. It had just been opened for use. Designed by Charles Coolidge Haight, it was the third of a group built by him on the block between Forty-ninth and Fiftieth Streets and Madison and Fourth Avenues, which was devoted to the trains of the New York Central Railroad with their smoke-belching, bell-ringing engines. In this block the old college building, called by the boys the "Maison de Punk," and the house of the President (then Frederick A. P. Barnard) had stood alone. The new building, something between Romanesque and Gothic in style, partly stone and partly brick, with iron beams in the roof of the great reading room and incandescent electric lights (the first in the city), was monumental in character and noteworthy as one of the first in a new school of architecture in New York. The reading room was nobly proportioned, lofty, and well lighted by day as well as by night, but, as was usually the case with architects and librarians, they had made no provision for extension for the storage of books and there was no possible means of expansion.

11

The staff of the Library, when the class arrived (i.e. in 1884), consisted of the "Librarians of Departments," William G. Baker, an old gentleman with white hair, perfectly dressed in a frock coat and immaculate linen, who presided over the law books in the east end of the reading room; George Hall Baker, afterwards, on Melvil Dewey's retirement, Librarian of the University, who looked after the books in "political economy" and history in the west end of the room; Walter Stanley Biscoe, who came from Amherst with Mr. Dewey as the head of the classification division; Harry Lyman Koopman, later Librarian of Brown University, who had charge of the cataloguing; and William James Terwilliger, who was in charge of the loans.

There were "assistants" too, all young women, much to the joy of the Campus. When Mr. Dewey came to Columbia, he brought with him a group of six Wellesley College graduates, partly for the help they were to give and partly to emphasize his contention that library work offered a special field for women, even in a men's college. These ladies were all delightful, and all eventually gave up library work to be married!

The class itself consisted of some ten or twelve men and women, of all sorts and kinds, eager to become librarians, some of them later to be distinguished in that profession.

Lectures were given by Mr. Dewey, Mr. George Baker, and Mr. Biscoe in the office of the Chief Librarian, a box of a place opening off the reading room, where the class sat in a crowded circle. In his report of 1886 Mr. Dewey says: "During the two years there have been weekly lectures or conferences, usually by the Chief Librarian, on various topics in Library Economy and Bibliography. . . . All of this is, of course, preliminary to our school of Library Economy to be opened next January [1887]."

The talks were really on all manner of subjects, without any particular plan, but calculated to bring home to the students the philosophy of the new library ideas, correct administration, and efficient methods of work. All the obvious things, cataloguing, accessioning, Cutter tables, classifying, etc., were discussed, but the subjects that stand out in my mind as receiving much time were those in which the Chief Librarian was particularly interested — standardization of sizes of cards, slips, paper, shelves, bookcases, and quality and durability; economy of space in cards and guides; shelf labels, book supports, charging systems, bulletin boards and bulletin-board material, colors, shelf lists; binding; the metric system; and simplified spelling. These were the days when the inventions and gadgets of the Library Bureau, founded by Dewey, were revelations, when catalogue cards were written by hand, all sorts and kinds of hands, and it was a proud day when the "Library Hand," the model set by Miss Carrie F. Pierce of our group (later of the Wellesley College Library), was printed by the Library Bureau and put into general use. It was now, too, that the typewriter, the Hammond, was experimented with for typing cards, and another proud event was the invention by Mrs. J. E. Dixon of our own class of the red

13

and black ribbon. There was no talk in the meetings about fine bindings, only the practical things, buckram and skiver; no discussion on typography, only about legibility of types; while the matters of interest to the bibliophile and collector were ignored.

All the members of the class were put to work in the Library, under the direction of the assistant librarians, Mr. Biscoe and Mr. Koopman. In his report for 1886, Mr. Dewey says: "When the library was reorganized, I proposed that we should attempt the general cataloguing, arrangement, numbering, etc., of the 50,000 volumes in the first three years, besides carrying on the regular work. To do this involved unusual efforts, but it is gratifying to find at the end of these three years, that we have more than kept up to our initial estimates."

The class helped to accomplish this remarkable task. Each member was given a chance to accession, catalogue, classify, and shelf-list; and when it was found that he or she had a particular aptitude for this or that kind of task, the chance was given for continuation as a paid assistant, a member of the staff. Thus training and practice united in their perfect work. In the report for 1886, the names of many of the class appear in the list of the staff, among them Miss Mary Salome Cutler as cataloguer, a position she occupied until she began her distinguished career in the real Library School, as Mrs. Fairchild.

It is hard at this date to understand what a strange new thing the founding of a library school was. When Dewey presented the idea to a meeting of the American Library Association in 1883, support was by no means complete or unqualified. W. F. Poole, of Poole's Index fame, felt that information about library work could not be conveyed by lectures, that there was "no training-school for educating librarians like a well-managed library," and that the larger libraries should teach cataloguers. "I do not wish to throw cold water upon the scheme," he continued — but at this point his objections were interrupted by the quick wit of Guy A. Brown, who remarked, "It seems to me that the gentleman has thrown a whole pool."[2]

The class of 1885 helped settle the question as to whether or not librarianship could be taught in a school. Looking back, I believe we of that group helped to encourage the Trustees of Columbia, infected by the enthusiasm of Melvil Dewey, to proceed with the establishment of the Library School, opened January 5, 1887, because we must have shown plainly that the plan could be made to work.

What Dewey taught was not the love of books, either for their literary content or their physical properties, but how to administer a library and how to care for the needs of those who would know and use books. His adoption of the word "Economy," somewhat strange sounding at the time, expressed exactly what he had in mind — the administration of a library in a business-like, efficient manner.

Dewey was one of those who put the public library on the map with the public school as one of the great educational agencies; he did more than anyone else to give libraries a uniformity and a professional character, with laws and machinery for their administra-

15

tion. He had his peculiarities, but his amusing desire to reform the spelling of the English language was shared by President Barnard of Columbia and should not be held against him, considering the reasonable and admirable things he did, including his advocacy of the metric system. His plan for the training of librarians was the first attempt of the kind in this country and was quickly followed in other colleges and places. He was not a great student or scholar, nor a great bibliographer, but he was what may be called a great mechanician. He knew instinctively what was needed to make the library machine a good one.

Dewey stood for the dignity of his profession, librarianship, and for the importance of the public library as second only to the public school as a source for the education of the people. He stood for the enjoyment by all libraries of the same privileges and machinery. He believed in the solidarity of the system, and he was active in the organization of the American Library Association. He was the founder and for a time editor of the library organ, the *Library Journal.* He invented the decimal system for the classification of books, thereby making it possible for the ordinary person to do such classification. Long afterwards, an assistant I had had in the Norwich Academy Library, Dorcas Fellows, at my suggestion went to the Albany Library School, and became the editor of the decimal classification, a position she held for the rest of her life.

Dewey drew up rules for cataloguing which in effect codified all such rules. Previous to his activities, each
library in the country was sufficient unto itself, with

little or no relationship with other libraries. There were a few distinguished librarians, but their whole time and energy were given to their own work. Dewey with his inventions and organizations changed all that.

No one except John Cotton Dana was so prolific in ideas for the aggrandizement of libraries and librarians, but even Dana benefited by what Dewey had done before him. The work done by these men in making the library one of the great educational forces had greater influence than any attempt of museums to become a similar force. For one reason, librarians, following Dewey's lead, are trained first of all as public servants. Museum curators, museum directors, are not so trained, and few of them seem to have imbibed the notion of the importance of that relationship.

What the Columbia School taught me, what I had not known before, were the things that Dewey himself stood for and that, I think I may say, I saw him accomplish. My training as a librarian was of the greatest value to me, especially the courses in organization and bibliography and the training in public relationships, helping me, when the opportunity came, to do for the Metropolitan Museum what was considered essential for a public agency.

As a boy, I had always wanted to be an architect but, not having the time to study for that profession, nor the money required for such study, I had given up the idea and had taken up what seemed to me the next best thing. My interest, however, continued, and while at Columbia I attended the public lectures on architecture which were given by Professor William R. Ware, 17 head of the Department of Architecture and a Trustee of the newly founded Metropolitan Museum of Art. Ware firmly established the Beaux-Arts system of education in the Massachusetts Institute of Technology and is called by W. H. Kilham in his book on Boston architecture, *Boston after Bulfinch,* "the founder of American architectural education." Discussing the matter with him one day, I owe him my thanks for his suggestion that public art museums, then being founded and bound to grow in number and importance, would need young men to serve them. Why didn't I, he said, try museum work as an alternative field for my endeavor?

About this time (it was in the 1880's), Edward Robinson, inspired by the lectures and influence of Charles Eliot Norton, who taught the humanities at Harvard, went to Germany and Greece to continue his studies of Greek art and archaeology. After having followed courses in Berlin and excavating in Greece, he came home to Boston, where he was employed by its museum as the first Curator of Classical Antiquities, and later as Director. I did not think myself in Robinson's class, of course, but his enthusiasm fired me, gave me ideas, and afterwards, when I came to know him, he helped me in many ways. He and Professor Ware fixed my mind to become a "museum worker," though I still went on in the Library to earn my living until a museum job should offer, until museum trustees began to appreciate that young men should be educated for such jobs.

18   In those days, the chief and perhaps the only thing

the American museum man thought about, of necessity, was the acquisition of objects to go in his museum,
objects of art — what to get, where to get them, and
what to pay for them. That appeared to be his only
duty. Fortunate for him and for his study was the
fact that just about this time there began to be a
general interest in the fine arts. Many books were now
appearing on the history of the arts — Charles C. Perkins was writing, and the artists William Morris Hunt,
William Wetmore Story, and John La Farge; a little
later, William A. Coffin, William C. Brownell, William H. Goodyear, Kenyon Cox, Russell Sturgis, and
others were publishing articles and books.[3] Dealers
in art were springing up everywhere, and, most important of all, the museums of Europe, especially in
Germany, were waking up to the importance of their
jobs. How to administer his museum, and all of the
matters time was to teach him, the museum man still
knew little about. Such problems were handled by his
Board of Trustees, who, being businessmen, did it
fairly well.

In the autumn of 1886, because of illness, I went to
Florida. There I planted orange trees and tried my
hand at teaching in a cracker school, where "disciplin"
was needed, the previous master having been run out
by the boys, who shot at a target behind his desk. In
March, 1888, I returned to the Columbia Library, in
the Card Catalogue Department, cataloguing the
Stephen Whitney Phoenix collection — a large and
valuable bequest covering many fields and notable
also for its handsome leather bindings — and the first

books on architecture that Samuel P. Avery, bene-
factor of Columbia and the New York Public Library,
gave for his great Avery Architectural Library, as a
memorial to his son. I also registered for some work
in the Library School, and thus it happens that I am
recorded as a member of the class of 1890, the group
of 1885, since it preceded the formal opening of the
School, never having been recognized as an official class.

Perhaps one should not make a reference that allows
people to compute the ages of one's friends, but it is
pleasant to me to remember Columbia's student body
as I met it, and especially certain ones who became
celebrated, like Nicholas Murray Butler, in his student
days called "the Dude," because he dressed better than
anyone else, and pretty Annie Nathan, afterwards
Mrs. Alfred Meyer, a student in Columbia's so-called
"Collegiate Course for Women," and, at about the
time that I left Columbia, the leader of those working
for the founding of Barnard College, which opened
in 1889. In her book, *Barnard Beginnings,* she speaks
of how Melvil Dewey, with his vigorous enthusiasm
for women's education, helped to start her off on her
courageous undertaking.

When I first went to Columbia, I lived in a flat kept
by an old lady, in a house overlooking the railroad
tracks on Fourth Avenue, next door to a brewery, and
I ate my dinners at a place frequented by brakemen
of the New York Central Road. As soon as I could
afford it, I went to a boarding house run by Madame
von Ettinger, a German baroness, on Forty-fifth Street,
over the railroad bridge. Paul Cravath, then in the

Columbia Law School, was living there to perfect his German, and Mary Salome Cutler, of the Library. Some of the institutions I was connected with in their early days have grown and waxed strong, but the boarding house seems to have disappeared from New York life, and it is amusing now to remember that that is how young men and women away from home commonly lived in those days.

Cravath became a tutor in the Law School and used to come into the Library, evenings, when his work was done, and sit and talk with a man who was a constant reader. I worked evenings. He said to me once, "Keep your eye peeled, and you'll see that man President of the United States some day." The man just missed it, but he did become the Chief Justice of the Supreme Court, did Charles Evans Hughes.

Suddenly, in 1888, I was offered a position in a place where I least expected it, in the Free Academy at Norwich, Connecticut, where I had been to school, as the Librarian of its Peck Library and the Curator of the newly established Slater Memorial Museum. My library training had helped me to get this job, Dewey recommended me, and the opportunity to study art and museums was now given me. Professor Ware had been ahead of his time in giving advice.

NOTES

Library Training in Boston and Columbia

[1] In recalling this period I have taken much from my paper, "Reminiscences of Early Days," given at the celebration of the fiftieth anniversary of the School and printed in the *Library Journal* (vol. 62, February 15, 1937, pp. 146-148).

[2] *Library Journal*, vol. 8, September-October, 1883, pp. 285-291, 293-295.

[3] John B. Montignani, "A Note on the Bibliography of Art: Some XIX Century American Authors," *Bulletin of The Metropolitan Museum of Art*, vol. 36, January, 1941, pp. 12-16.

The NORWICH FREE

ACADEMY *&* *The* SLATER

MEMORIAL BUILDING

THE SLATER MEMORIAL MUSEUM at the time of its opening in 1888 and for a decade or so thereafter had an important place in the then rather small new world of American museums and American art education. It was unusual, if not indeed unique, in being a school museum, in the sense that it was given to and operated by the Norwich Free Academy; at the same time, its reach and its reputation gave it a place among institutions designed to serve the general public. The history of its foundation is worth recounting, too, because there came together in its inception three large-statured men: the generous and kindly donor, Mr. William A. Slater, ever ready to help open up along a wide front educational opportunities in his native city; President Daniel Coit Gilman, that great educator-executive, likewise Norwich born, whose impress may be found on institutions educational, medical,   2 3 charitable, artistic, in Connecticut, California, Baltimore, Washington, and New York; and Dr. Robert Porter Keep, principal of the Norwich Free Academy from 1885 to 1902, who made of the Academy in his day "a university of secondary education."[1]

The early history of the Norwich Free Academy is not without significance for our story, for it suggests what manner of institution this was that within less than four years could acquire a museum, a normal school, an art school, and a manual training department, and which served as a cultural center for the community.

The lively hero of the Academy's founding was Dr. John Putnam Gulliver, minister of the Broadway Congregational Church from 1845 to 1865. About 1846 the public elementary schools of Norwich had fallen upon evil days, and a group of educationally minded, public-spirited citizens, among them Dr. Gulliver, made a long and strenuous effort over a period of years to bring about reform. They met with so much opposition — demagogism is the word used in contemporary reports — that for the time being they abandoned all attempts at direct reform. The idea was in the air, however, that a good secondary school, open to all, might raise the level of the lower schools; and when Dr. Gulliver undertook singlehandedly to raise funds for an endowed academy which should furnish secondary education to the boys and girls of Norwich, rich and poor alike, this hope was ever present in his mind. A publicly owned, tax-supported high school, it was felt, would be too subject to fluctuations in public and political thinking to keep a steady educational course. Tied to the ballot box, what was to prevent it from falling into the lamentable state of the lower schools? But a privately owned and controlled institution, offering superior education to all qualified students, it was thought, would make for public elementary schools able to turn out candidates capable of taking advantage of this opportunity. And, in fact, drastic reform of the public school system did follow immediately upon the incorporation of the Academy in 1854, as a result of general public pressure and under the aegis of the former opposition.

Norwich was a city of substantial fortunes, and its wealthy citizens not at all obtuse to educational interests; nevertheless, Dr. Gulliver's attempt to raise $75,000 for the endowment of an academy was no light matter. In a speech made at the dedication of the Slater Memorial building over thirty years later he gives some of the details, and by his account this campaign in decorous New England of the fifties appears to have been as arduous as money-raising habitually is. For two years Dr. Gulliver labored, approaching prospective donors individually, securing conditional pledges, and carefully avoiding any general appeal. When three pledges of $7,500 were in hand, he asked General William Williams to put in a five-acre piece of land as a site for the school, at a valuation of $7,500, conditional as always upon the raising of the sum of $75,000. He waited months for a decision, until Mrs. Williams, later the donor of the school library, intervened in his behalf. The well-chosen site, still occupied by the Academy, lies between Norwichtown and the center of the city, but within the city limits. The school field and the small wooded hill behind the buildings were in my day greatly treasured by the students.

Finally the campaign stuck at $68,000, and the thirty-odd surprised subscribers were called together. Dr. Gulliver humorously reports "groanings" as they were reminded of their promises; nevertheless, the amount was brought up to $76,450, and in 1854 the Norwich Free Academy was incorporated by thirty-five subscribers and the valiant Dr. Gulliver. Later, when more money was needed for the building, another $10,000 was raised, and the number of subscribers brought up to forty.[2] The Academy opened on October 21, 1856, with eighty students in the first term. Of these anxieties, ingenuities, and machinations Miss Caulkins in her *History of Norwich* has little to say; she has her own way of reporting how the Academy, of which the town was so proud, had come into being. "This establishment," she writes, "is a magnificent illustration of what can be accomplished by enlightened forethought, persevering enterprise, and large-hearted liberality."[3]

The purpose of the Academy[4] was "to provide, for all classes in the community, an education adequate to all the demands of their future occupations" — a large order, surely, but at least not one to cramp the development of the school. Young ladies were to be educated "to adorn society, to mould the mind of youth, to be the honored heads of well-ordered households and to charm by the beauty of an elegant culture and a disciplined mind." Boys were to be prepared for college

26

or polytechnic school, or, if they did not intend further education, for business and trades, not so much by direct vocational work as by general training in underlying principles. To these ends the three courses, Classical, Scientific, and General, were directed. Originally the "young ladies" were considered a fourth, and separate, group, but they soon came to take their places in the other courses, according to their abilities and plans for the future.

The standing of the Academy was always exceedingly high. The boys of the Classical and Scientific Courses went, normally, to Yale, and at one time it was said that only Phillips Academy in Andover sent students as well prepared.[5] The reputation of the Academy always brought to it a number of students from other places, who paid a nonresident fee and boarded in the town.

In structure, the Academy continues today as it began — a private, incorporated institution serving as the public high school for the city and surrounding towns.

The Peck Library, of which I was to be Librarian, came into existence with the founding of the school, although it moved into new quarters with the opening of the museum building. Like the Academy itself, it owed much to the "persevering enterprise" of Dr. Gulliver, so talented in exciting "large-hearted liberality." He told me once the following story which he said I was to remember, and you see I have. He approached Mrs. Harriet Peck Williams, whose husband had already given the land for the Academy, suggesting that she give a library to the school as a memorial to her distinguished father, Captain Bela Peck, who had pre-

27

served his interest in public affairs until his death in his ninety-third year. She told him she would consider the matter, and to come again for her answer. This he did, and she said she had decided to give the Library, but only on one condition, and that was that when he died, he should plan to have his funeral service preached from the text, "And it came to pass that the beggar died." He, being quick on the trigger, replied, "Yes, but with the rest of the verse, 'and was carried by the angels into Abraham's bosom.' " The laugh was on the lady, especially if one remembers the rest of the story and what happened to the rich man. Mrs. Williams, in any case, gave two gifts to the Library of $5,000 each, as well as $1,000 for the initial purchase of books and about the same amount for the furnishings of the room, and the Library she endowed became one of the finest school libraries in the country. It was said to have been the first endowed library of a secondary school in New England. An early account mentions 145 volumes of the *Bibliotheca Classica* and the *Edinburgh* and *Quarterly Reviews* from their beginnings — stiff reading for high school students, we should think now. When I went to it, it was particularly rich in the classics, botany, English literature, and works of reference.

For well on toward thirty years, the original Academy building stood alone on its five-acre site. But the school was growing, according to the nature of healthy organisms, and Principal Hutchison saw that an additional building was greatly needed. His was the honor of receiving from Mr. William Slater the promise of a new building for the school, but not the joy of seeing the completed edifice or the excitement of working out plans for the fullest use of it. Nevertheless, as the Academy catalogue of 1885-86 said, "The last term of his labors was brightened by the prospect of the new facilities which this splendid gift would secure to the school." The building was far enough advanced in June, 1886, to accommodate the graduation exercises, though the dedication ceremony did not take place until November 4 of that year.

In the entrance porch to the building, a dignified bronze tablet recounts simply:

THIS BUILDING
DEDICATED TO THE EDUCATION OF THE YOUNG
AND COMMEMORATIVE OF
JOHN F. SLATER
IS ERECTED BY HIS SON
WILLIAM A. SLATER
AND BY HIM PRESENTED TO THE
NORWICH FREE ACADEMY
IN GRATEFUL RECOGNITION
OF ADVANTAGES THERE ENJOYED

The speakers at the dedication exercises had a good deal more to say — about the Slater family, about the history of the Academy, about the possible uses of the building. Dr. Gulliver grandly reminded his audience that "the blended sagacity and generosity which the immediate donor has written in our sight over these beautiful walls and built into this monumental structure is itself in part an inheritance. It is the blossoming

29

of a century-plant."[6] In truth, the Slater family had
figured importantly in the American scene ever since,
in 1789, Samuel Slater, great-uncle of William, had
arrived from England, bringing the designs of the
new cotton machinery of Arkwright, Hargreaves, and
Crompton, not on paper, which was against the law,
but "in his head." Some years later his younger brother
John, grandfather of William, also emigrated from
England, bringing in the same manner the latest de-
velopments in machinery for making yarns and cloths.
John Fox Slater (1815-1884), in whose memory the
building was erected, successfully continuing the family textile industry, had given a million dollars for the
education of the freedmen in 1882, the first great gift
of money in this country except the Peabody Fund.
When the history of emancipation was written, said
Daniel Coit Gilman, three Norwich names would be
included: "a teacher who devoted his life to their [the
Negroes'] instruction [Edmund A. Ware]; a senator
who pleaded that education should go hand in hand
with citizenship [Lafayette S. Foster]; and a philanthro-
pist who gave liberally and wisely to secure this end
[John F. Slater]."[7] Dr. Gulliver's claim of "grasp and
concentration of mind" and "discriminating benefi-
cence" as family characteristics was no mere flattery of
a rich donor. "Only a man of large mind can devise
large things," said President Gilman, "only a man of
resolution and a strong sense of duty can execute a
noble purpose."[8] He spoke with authority, as one of the
original trustees of the Slater Fund and also as one who
30 had himself devised and executed large enterprises.

William A. Slater, the "immediate donor," instead of following the usual procedure of Academy graduates and going to Yale, had gone to Harvard. There he fell under the spell of Charles Eliot Norton and the interest in art he preached and awakened. A collector himself of the painters then popular, chiefly the Barbizon School, Mr. Slater, after his marriage, lived a great deal in Europe, at Biarritz, where he had a house, but he kept up his interest in Norwich and in artistic matters all his life, even after he went to Washington to live, and he was quick to help along any project that seemed to open up educational possibilities in his native city. By all the incidents of his life he was fitted to be called a "first citizen" — by his gifts to the church, to the local hospital, and to the school of his boyhood. He was the kindest and most generous of men, and he was fortunate in the character of his advisers: Charles Eliot Norton, his teacher; William Hutchison and Robert Porter Keep, the principals of the school; and Daniel Coit Gilman — all men of unusual sympathy and character.

In July, 1885, while the Slater Memorial was being built, Dr. Robert Porter Keep had come to the Norwich Free Academy as its third principal, and it seems to have been Dr. Keep who first had the notion of setting up in the new building a museum of casts. Dr. Keep was a Greek scholar of rank, author of several textbooks in the field, including the widely used *Greek Lessons* and Autenrieth's *Homeric Dictionary,* which he translated with additions and corrections. A graduate and Ph.D. of Yale, he had been United States Consul

31

at Piraeus, and had then spent three years in research
in Germany and Italy, living for some months in Berlin with Ernst Curtius, the historian of Greece. For
nine years before he came to Norwich he had been
teaching Greek in Williston Seminary. Although Greek
was his passion and association with a small group of
philologists one of his private joys, Dr. Keep was no
mere grammarian. He came from a family of educators
— his father had been a teacher in the American Asy-
lum for the Deaf and Dumb in Hartford; his uncle was
President Noah Porter of Yale; his aunt, Miss Sarah
Porter, had a School for Girls at Farmington — and he
had large designs for the development of the Academy.[9]

The idea of a museum in the new building was developed during 1886 by correspondence between Dr.
Keep and Mr. Slater, then in Europe.[10] Dr. Keep's notion fell on soil apparently made fertile by the evange-
listic teaching of Charles Eliot Norton, whose single
influence in all the Boston orbit was still immense.
Then, at the dedication of the building, on November
4, 1886, tentative plans were projected in the address
of President Daniel Coit Gilman.

"Mr. Slater has not told me what to say," said the
President of Johns Hopkins University, "and I am not
even sure that he will approve of every phrase I may
employ; but he has expressed his own ideas so clearly
in the arrangement, the construction, the position, and
the name of this academic hall, that it is an easy as well
as a pleasant task to translate into speech the hopes and
purposes already recorded in bricks and stones."[11]

After suggesting the use of the lecture hall for public

lectures and readings and music, the use of the class-
rooms for courses, open to interested townspeople, in
"history, literature, the fine arts," and for conferences
and small meetings, and the opening of the Peck Library to the public two or three hours every afternoon,
he went on to advise the establishment of a museum of
the fine arts. "South Kensington has taught us that reproductions in plaster and in electrotype can be secured
from almost all the great museums of the world. To an
ordinary observer these reproductions, in form, color,
inscriptions, are as instructive as the originals. . . . Such
museums have already been begun in several American
cities. It will not be best to copy any one of them, but
rather to give to the Academy Museum a character of
its own, so choice and so instructive that the virtuosos
from other places will come here to study it. A valuable
accessory will be a collection of the autotypes of Braun,
and other photographs, which should not be impris-
oned in a portfolio, but so displayed that everybody
may see them."[12]

What President Gilman had to say was certainly not
dictated by Mr. Slater, and it was perhaps a diplomatic
bit of wishful thinking to imply that the building itself
suggested a museum, for it was generally known that
no idea of a museum entered into the original plan of
the building. President Gilman was apparently speaking for Dr. Keep on behalf of a project they had discussed together and agreed upon. Two letters from
President Gilman to Dr. Keep, preserved in the Slater
Memorial Museum, make this plain. The first, dated
October 25, 1886, asks that Dr. Keep look over the

address so that he may have the opportunity to make any modifications he wishes. "In general," the letter goes on, "I shall talk about the future of our New England towns, — a general theme which enables me to bring in several of the particulars to which allusion was made in our recent interview. I shall try to help on the good foundation . . . which you have in charge. . . . I shall be very grateful for any hint in advance."

Apparently Dr. Keep replied with an expression of confidence in Dr. Gilman, for the second letter, dated October 29, says, "There is no danger that I shall not be in accord with you but still as we have an end in view, it is well that our phrases should be guarded." He then makes arrangements to see Dr. Keep after his arrival in Norwich and before the hour of the speech.

President Gilman's great achievements in the organization of the hospital and the medical school at Johns Hopkins have lately been so ably brought to mind[13] that it is astonishing to find him speaking with so much authority, now and later at the opening of the Museum, on matters of art. Yet it was not a new field for this versatile educator. Nearly thirty years before, in 1858, as Librarian of Yale, he had planned Yale's first temporary art exhibition, over two hundred paintings assembled from private collections in Connecticut and New York. This exhibition, designed especially "to awaken and gratify a love of the Fine Arts, among the students of the college, and the residents of the town," drew spectators also from a wider area, for the railroads offered half fare to attenders at the exhibition — a fact which no doubt increased the prestige of the exhibition in its

34

own locality. Out of Dr. Gilman's efforts at Yale came the gift by Augustus Russell Street of funds for a School of Fine Arts, and in Street Hall, completed in 1866, was deposited the celebrated James Jackson Jarves collection of early Italian paintings.[14]

The Slater Memorial building, so auspiciously dedicated with ceremonies reviewing the past of the institution to which it was given and suggesting the uses to which it might be put, was in itself a source of great pride to the school and the town. The Academy catalogue of 1889-90 describes it as follows:

"This edifice was dedicated November 4, 1886. It measures 150 feet, by 68 feet, and has a round tower 145 feet in height. It contains, on the lower floor, a large hall for public and anniversary occasions, and two smaller halls, or class-rooms, which can be thrown into the large hall and increase its capacity to . . . 1,000 persons. The second and third stories are occupied by a magnificent Museum Hall, one of the finest interiors in the country; by an exquisite library-room, to which the Peck Library has been transferred; and by two class-rooms. The materials used in finishing the interior are hard-wood and marble. As respects solidity of construction and perfection of finish, the Memorial Building is unsurpassed in New England."

Almost from the opening of the building, the use of the lecture hall and the classrooms was in accord with President Gilman's suggestions. I shall speak in later chapters of some of the activities that went on there in the field of art. Under Dr. Keep's discriminating guidance there were also well-known lecturers on other sub-

35

jects, excellent music, such as the Beethoven String Quartette, and small study groups in various subjects, for instance, graduate classes in French and German. The building quickly became, in effect, a sort of athenaeum and lyceum for the town.

NOTES

[1] In the Academy catalogue of 1893-94 this phrase is attributed to Dr. John Putnam Gulliver; it has also been assigned to President Gilman (*Dictionary of American Biography,* vol. X, p. 286).

[2] In *American Journal of Education,* vol. 2, December, 1856, pp. 665-700, and vol. 3, March, 1857, pp. 191-212, there is a full contemporary account of the founding of the Norwich Free Academy, with all the inaugural addresses, including one by Dr. Gulliver. The livelier details of his fund-raising campaign, however, come in a "now it can be told" address nearly thirty years later, at the dedication of the Slater Memorial building on November 4, 1886 — *Addresses Delivered at the Dedication of the Slater Memorial Building* . . . by Professor John Putnam Gulliver and President Daniel Coit Gilman, Cambridge, Mass.: John Wilson and Son, University Press, 1887.

[3] Frances Manwaring Caulkins, *History of Norwich, Connecticut: From Its Possession by the Indians, to the Year 1866,* [Hartford, Conn.]: Published by the author, 1866, p. 549.

[4] *American Journal of Education,* vol. 2, pp. 689-693.

[5] Professor Thacher, quoted by Leonard Woolsey Bacon in his article on Norwich, *New England Magazine,* n.s. vol. 15, October, 1896, p. 180.

[6] *Addresses . . . at the Dedication of the Slater Memorial Building* . . . by Professor John Putnam Gulliver and President Daniel Coit Gilman, pp. 6-7.

[7] *Op. cit.,* p. 33.

[8] *Op. cit.,* p. 32.

[9] Dr. Keep's daughter, Mrs. Robert L. Hale, has kindly supplemented from her personal knowledge the information in Claude M. Fuess's article on Robert Porter Keep in the *Dictionary of American Biography,* New York: Charles Scribner's Sons, 1933, vol. X, pp. 286-287.

Mr. Henry A. Tirrell, a favorite pupil of Dr. Keep's at the Academy and later his successor as principal, has also generously helped with his recollections.

[10] "The Slater Museum Done," *New-York Daily Tribune,* November 22, 1888, p. 2, and Dr. Keep's own address at the Museum opening, as reported in the Norwich *Bulletin,* November 23, 1888.

[11] Gilman, *Addresses . . .* , p. 31.

[12] *Op. cit.,* pp. 40-41.

[13] Abraham Flexner, *Daniel Coit Gilman: Creator of the American Type of University.* New York: Harcourt, Brace and Company, [1946].

[14] I am indebted for these facts about President Gilman's early ventures in art to Wilmarth S. Lewis, *The Yale Collections,* New Haven: Yale University Press, 1946, pp. 16-17. More than a decade after the opening of the Slater Museum, President Gilman was also active in the organization of the Municipal Art Society of Baltimore.

OPENING OF THE SLATER

MEMORIAL MUSEUM

THE SLATER MEMORIAL BUILDING was erected and in use; the donor of the building made an additional gift to cover the cost of the museum; and on March 23, 1887, Edward Robinson, then in charge of the classical collections in the Boston Museum of Fine Arts, accepted the appointment to select, purchase, and install the contents of the Slater Memorial Museum.

The museum was to be entirely a museum of reproductions, but of reproductions treated with the gravity and respect due their great originals. The selection was made with "extreme care"; an article in the *Nation* of August 16, 1888, possibly by Russell Sturgis, went so far as to say of the classical part of the collection: "It does not appear that it would be possible to choose better the same number of pieces as representative of the whole mass of such sculpture which is known to us moderns. If any piece not included were proposed, on condition of excluding one of the present collection to make room for it, it would be seen that such a change would be of at least doubtful expediency."[1]

The same informed taste went into the arrangement,   39

which took thought for the two needs of museum display — on the one hand, study, understanding, the intellectual processes; on the other, the direct, immediate experience of the work of art. The basic chronological arrangement was there so that "the successive stages in the progress of sculpture, or in other words, the different schools and the characteristics of each school, reveal themselves to the observant and thoughtful visitor."[2] The knowing could speak of "the great Eleusis relief being more perfectly placed and illuminated, for all purposes of examination and study, than any copy of this important and puzzling work of art that we can now recall in Europe" and of the Nike of Paionios "shown here, as nowhere else in the world, on an exact reproduction of its original pedestal."[3] What was probably more important for inexperienced visitors was the studied effort to give these masterpieces a chance to make their own impression. Here was nothing of the "dirty old casts huddled together." Curtains of heavy raw silk, maroon in color, separated the main floor into compartments, with a few carefully placed pieces in each — these compartments surrounding the large central hall, devoted to bigger groups. "Beautiful and orderly and serene — a very lovely place," so one of the art students remembers it, after years of experience in one of the country's greatest museums.

In the main hall were displayed the Hermes of Praxiteles; eight figures from the east pediment of the Parthenon, representing the birth of Athena; reliefs from the great altar of Pergamon, extending well across the room; five figures from the western pediment of the

The Slater Memorial Museum in Norwich

Main hall of the Slater Memorial Museum

Temple of Zeus at Olympia; the Victory of Paionios on a reproduction of its original three-sided pedestal; the Victory of Samothrace; a selection of the slabs of the frieze of the Parthenon, all round the room; and various other casts. In the balconies were the baptismal font by Jacopo della Quercia, from the Baptistery of Saint John in Siena; the base of one of the flagpoles in front of Saint Mark's, Venice; the Saint George of Donatello; the pulpit of Santa Croce in Florence by Benedetto da Maiano; Michelangelo's Moses and the tomb of the Medici; and the twelve Apostles by Peter Vischer, in Nuremberg. The total number of casts of Greek sculpture and architecture was 124; of Italian, 103.

Besides the casts, there were electrotype reproductions of Greek coins, plaster reproductions of some of the smaller arts of the Renaissance, and 581 photographs of paintings and European architecture. Some two hundred and fifty of the photographs were exhibited on screens in one of the galleries, in individual frames. These had removable backs, so that the photographs on exhibition could be frequently changed — a feature which, like the revolving pedestals for the sculpture, was comparatively, if not entirely, new at the time in this country.

Adjoining the Slater Memorial Museum was a beautiful room, with fine light and a timbered roof, where the Peck Library was now installed.

A school of high standing and distinguished history, a building considered one of the finest in New England, a collection "unsurpassed, perhaps unequalled, by any that is owned by any college in the land,"[4] an installation guided by rare taste, knowledge, and skill — such was the institution to which I came as Curator and Librarian a few days before the formal opening of the Slater Memorial Museum on November 22, 1888.

Almost at once, I had my initiation into the kind of gusty crisis that helps to keep a museum man's course from becoming too smooth. Somebody, somehow, had at the last moment thrown up horrified hands at the unconcealed naturalism of the Greek sculpture that was going to be displayed on the morrow. Cico, the plasterer, was called to the rescue with a sheaf of proper if hastily made fig leaves, and, after a bit of rushing round, the Museum was ready to be opened with, it was hoped, irreproachable dignity. A month later, some of the New York and Boston newspapers raised a hullaballoo about this desecration of pure art, with appropriate sneers at provincial prudery, but Norwich stood its ground.

The opening was in fact a very grand occasion, worth recounting in some detail these nearly sixty years later because it shows both the prestige the Museum had at its beginning and the particular impetus the new Curator was to receive in a direction which he was to pursue both here and at the Metropolitan.

Visitors from Boston and Cambridge came by special train, in Mr. Slater's private car, arriving at noon. They were duly escorted to the Slater building, where they were given "ample refreshments" and opportunity to look at the Museum. The guests from New York arrived at two, and were hurried to the Museum that "they might examine the works of art there under the most favorable light." We find among distinguished guests mentioned in the various newspaper accounts of the occasion: President Eliot and Professors Allen, Wright, and Barrett Wendell of Harvard; Martin Brimmer, the first president of the Boston Museum; General Francis A. Walker, economist, statistician, and President of the Massachusetts Institute of Technology; General Charles G. Loring of the Boston Museum; E. H. Clement, Editor of the Boston *Transcript;* E. M. Wheelwright, Secretary of the Boston Society of Architects; W. P. P. Longfellow, the architect; Mrs. John L. Gardner and Mrs. Henry Whitman, Boston's vivid patronesses of art; Miss Shafer, President of Wellesley; N. P. Gilman of the *Literary World;* Professors Weir, Peck, and Seymour of Yale; Professor Poland of Brown; Dr. Gulliver (the Academy's brilliantly successful beggar), now of Andover Theological Seminary; D. W. Abercrombie, Principal of the Worcester Academy; Professor William R. Ware of Columbia, who had first suggested museum work to me; H. K. Jesup, Walter H. Lewis, and J. H. Twachtman, the artist, all of New York.

Elegantly dressed in a new black coat and striped trousers, I helped to seat these distinguished visitors, whose names were familiar to me if not their faces. I was overawed by their superiority and condescension.

The exercises began at 2:30, with prayer. Dr. Keep then recounted briefly the history of the Museum: the development of its general outlines by correspondence between him and Mr. Slater in 1886, President Gilman's support in the dedicatory address, advice from Professor Niemeyer of Yale and General Loring of the

Boston Museum, and the particular responsibility of Mr. Edward Robinson for the lovely finished achievement. "To those who know Mr. Robinson it is superfluous to praise his thorough knowledge of pure conception, his deep feeling for its beauty, his scrupulous exactness and his untiring industry. I do not hesitate to claim for him, too, great originality of conception. I know of no other collection where the objects in the order in which they are disclosed so work upon the beholder as do the objects in our central rotunda."[5]

Dr. Keep also related how the orders for the casts had been sent out June 25, 1887, the casts had begun to arrive the following autumn, carpenters and plasterers had started work in March, 1888, and the last case had arrived the Monday preceding the Thursday opening. He spoke pleasantly, too, of the "infinite ability and skill" with which the casts had been put together by the plasterer Giovanni Lugini, called "Cico," "a man with the frame of an athlete and the heart of an artist." For Dr. Keep, the beauty of the sculpture was a bond with the civilization it represented — "the hosts of Greeks who on the plain of Olympia, at the great festivals, have admired the Victory of Paionios and the Hermes of Praxiteles" and "the Greek girls who have gazed in dread and wonder at the Pallas Giustiniani, or the Venus of Milo."

The main speaker of the day was Charles Eliot Norton. George William Curtis had first been asked, and the invitation was held open for some weeks, Norton having been requested to urge its acceptance. Charles Eliot Norton himself, however, seems an almost inevitable choice. Appointed in 1874 "Lecturer on the History of the Fine Arts as Connected with Literature" at Harvard and later made its first professor of the fine arts, he was the one to whom everybody looked to talk about art, before everybody else began to talk about it. William Slater had taken his courses, so had Edward Robinson, and while Mr. Gilman could be counted on to talk about practical things, especially knowing his Norwich as well as he did, Mr. Norton's name carried more weight in his subject than that of anyone else, at least in New England.

Mr. Norton's oracular pronouncements were to leave me somewhat uncomprehending, to my distress, because they seemed to show me how little I knew, and his critical point of view offended my young optimism. But reading his address now[6] after all these years, when time and the critics have made plainer both his weaknesses and his achievements, I can see why I failed to get a great deal of guidance in my chosen profession from the speech of the pundit of arts who hailed from Boston. Many of the characteristics his critics have spoken of show up plainly in it — his New Englandism and his aestheticism, his scholarship and his evangelism, his exasperated scolding at America's lack of taste. The long discussion of the nature of art and its relation to morality, which takes up the first half of the address, illustrates aptly the temper of the Puritan preacher in him that Henry James was to point out at the time of Norton's death in 1908, noting how "a son of the Puritans the most intellectually transmuted, the most liberally emancipated and initiated possible, could still 45 plead most for substance when proposing to plead for style...."[7] Norton's conclusion "that beauty is the final end of the fine arts, and that, in accomplishing this end, it is as impossible to exclude morality from the work as it is to exclude it from the expression of character in conduct" shows him trying, in James's phrase, "to lose himself in the labyrinth of delight while keeping tight hold of the clue of duty."

The theme of the second half of Mr. Norton's address bears a more obvious relation to the opening of a school museum in an industrial community. Briefly stated, and stripped of such confusing red herrings as that the "end of education is ... the development of character" and "unless the artist be a superior man ... his work, whatever technical excellence it may exhibit, will be of an inferior order," the argument is that the love of beauty and the production of beautiful things are the final measure of civilization and that special culture of the imagination (i.e., education in these matters) is necessary for both appreciation and production of art.

Developing this theme, he of course characteristically noted that life in America — both its earlier austerities and its current materialism — was not conducive to artistic production. "There has not been as yet in America," he announced, "a single painter, sculptor or architect who has created a great work of art, who has succeeded in giving beautiful expression to the aspects and conditions of contemporary life, in forms that might define and complete the dim and imperfect ideals of this great, groping unimaginative commu-

46

nity." (Naturally the press found "there has not been as yet in America a single painter, sculptor or architect who has created a great work of art" a highly quotable statement, and it did not fail to appear in most of the press notices.)

Since America had not had time and culture to produce great works of art, so much the greater was the need of education directed to quickening the sensibilities, refining the taste, deepening the sympathies, and arousing and developing the love of beauty.

Particularly had the "great masses of our industrial population" need of such education, the dreariness of their lives having been increased by the prevalence of machine manufacture. No complete solution could be seen. "But," Norton's argument continued, "there are partial and imperfect means of improvement lying ready to our hands, and one of the most direct and powerful of them consists, strange as it may sound, in the culture of the love of beauty through the steady and intelligent culture of the imagination. Of the great mass of the products of toil for the support and service of life few have the quality of beauty, few are works of art in the sense of effort after perfection in execution. If we look at the articles in most common use, at our houses and the utensils and furniture with which they are filled, we cannot fail to see that few of these objects, however well they may answer to the purpose of mere utility, correspond with any idea of beauty or are fitted to give rational pleasure to the maker or the user. Fancy for an instant that we had as a nation beautiful houses, beautiful in simple and at the same time exquisite pro- 47 portions, filled with beautiful objects of common use, objects in the making of which the poetic faculties of the imagination had been employed; suppose that we took thought enough for beauty to demand it in carpet and wall-paper, in furniture and vessel, in jewellery and plate, in the thousand articles of use and adornment which we every day employ, — what increase in happiness would result from the exercise by the workman of his higher faculties in their production! It is you, it is I who, by acceptance of the ugly in place of the beautiful, are contributing to make the life of many a workman a life of deadening drudgery. It is you, it is I who, by cultivating our own faculties of perception and imagination so that they shall seek for gratification in the objects of commonest use, will help to quicken the perceptions and the imagination of their makers, and will occupy them in the production of things which it shall be an enjoyment to make and to use.

*   *   *

"It is as an attempt to provide means needed for the higher education of the community, it is as a school of the imagination, that we welcome this Museum of the Fine Arts, and celebrate its opening, and count it as the best gift that could be bestowed upon an educated and fortunate community."

Although I was unable to follow Mr. Norton's remarks with much sympathy or understanding, I did get, afterwards, his book on *Historical Studies of Church-Building in the Middle Ages,* which was of great service to me in my classes and seemed to make reasonable the place he occupied in public esteem as a teacher of art.

After Norton's speech of over an hour's length on "The Influence of Art and Its Relation to Morals," in a delivery "monotonous but pleasing," the announcement of President Daniel Coit Gilman's subject came with agreeable concreteness, "Greek Art in a Manufacturing Town of New England."[8]

Opening with a quotation from Sappho, President Gilman went on to a recollection of his own schooldays in the Academy of Calvin Tracy, which had preceded the Free Academy.

"When I remember how the Academy boys in my youth read their Rollin's Ancient History, and pored over the pages of old Lemprière, without so much as a marginal cut to aid their imagination, how photographs and casts were unknown, and the tale of a returning traveler was almost as rare as the voice of a nightingale, — and then turn to the wealth of illustrations collected beneath this roof — books, plates, photographs, casts, coins, and reproductions of ancient plate — a collection unsurpassed, perhaps unequalled, by any that is owned by any college in the land, the libation of admiration and gratitude is most heartily poured out. . . . A new intellectual force has been here introduced — destined to awaken, develop, and instruct the love of beauty. Consider what this means. 'The poetic passion, the desire of beauty, the love of art for art's sake, is most rewarding,' says Pater, 'for art comes to you professing to give nothing but the highest quality to your moments as they pass, and simply for those moments' sake.' "

Asking what the educational value of the Museum 49

would be, he noted that some young artists would be helped by the collections at the beginnings of their careers. But the Museum would also benefit directly a wider audience. "Here light is thrown upon the art, the architecture, the decorations, the coinage, the biography, the mythology, the religion of the most interesting epochs of the past. New interest will likewise be imparted to the study of ancient literature, whether the classics are read in their original form or in the masterly translations which modern scholarship has given us. Nor will this museum interpret ancient books alone. The visitor to these galleries will soon begin to ask for Winckelmann's History of Art, and for Lessing's Laocoon; Wordsworth's Greece, and the records of recent discoveries in Olympia, Mycenae, and Troy will be read with fresh interest; Ruskin, Taine, Pater, Symonds, Hamerton will be in demand; the Earthly Paradise will be revisited, and the Marble Faun will renew its youth; nor will the new volume of Lanciani, carried through the press by the same skillful hands that have arranged this museum, fail to be read, as it describes with the enthusiasm of an archaeological Columbus the discovery of sites and monuments unknown a few years since."

It is interesting to find in Gilman's address a quotation from the controversial "Conclusion" to Pater's *Renaissance,* which was published in the first edition in 1873, was withdrawn in the edition of 1877, and reappeared again in 1888; it sounds oddly like a thrust at Norton's moral ruminations. Interesting and curious, too, that it is Gilman and not Norton who mentions Ruskin and whom, from the paragraph just quoted, one might guess to be a teacher of the history of art, of literature, of the classics, where Norton, professor of the fine arts, from the text of his address seems more like a professor of philosophy discussing aesthetics without any close knowledge of recent art criticism and research. In general, Gilman's address gives the impression of coming from a much younger man, yet actually he was Norton's junior by only four years. His remarks concerning the interrelation of the museum and books now seem almost as if he were walking with the young Curator and Librarian from the Slater Museum hall to the beautiful Peck Library a few steps down the corridor, throwing out definite, helpful suggestions as they went. And you may be sure the Curator-Librarian pricked up his ears and took these words down in his mental notebook.

But President Gilman had still another point to make. "Another result," he went on, ". . . may be expected to follow this auspicious beginning — a result, less obvious, perhaps more subtle, than those before mentioned, but not less important, not less enduring. I allude to the influence of art upon industry." He reminded his audience that Norwich industry had prospered not because of nearness to the source of supplies but because of skill in using the products brought from a distance. He pointed out that competition was growing keener, from beyond the Alleghenies and south of Mason and Dixon's line. "In the future, beauty must be added to utility; to solidity, grace must be given; art must be allied to craft. Norwich must remember that the manufactures of Paris, Vienna, and Berlin spread the wide world over because they are so attractive. No amount of duties will exclude them. People who have the money will buy what they like, and the number of people who like the beautiful in form, in color, in material, and in decoration increases far more rapidly than the population."

"Perhaps at some future time," he went on, "Norwich may have an exhibition of 'Arts and Crafts' like that which has recently been held in London. Certainly to the promotion of Arts and Crafts the collections of the Slater Museum will tend. But let it not be forgotten that beyond the pleasure to be afforded to the purchaser, the pleasure to be afforded to the workman is incalculable. Upon this point, the impressive words of Professor Norton, to which we have just listened, need no emphasis from me. Let us take his admonitions home."

Impressing on his hearers the importance of improving the institutions devoted to higher education, he admonished the managers of the Academy to "enlarge its facilities, increase its staff of teachers, widen the opportunities to profit by this noble gift."

The positive approach of these remarks, the suggestion of things to be done, fired the imagination of a young man just entering a museum career, and gave him something he never forgot.

NOTES

[1] Vol. 47, p. 129.

[2] Introductory Note signed R[obert] P[orter] K[eep] and dated May, 1889, in Norwich Free Academy, *Catalogue and Brief Description of the Plaster Reproductions of Greek and Italian Sculpture in the Slater Memorial Museum, Norwich, Conn.*, Cambridge, Mass.: John Wilson and Son, University Press, 1889.

[3] *Nation, loc. cit.*

[4] Daniel C. Gilman, "Greek Art in a Manufacturing Town of New England: An Address Delivered at the Opening of the Slater Museum, Norwich, Connecticut." Reprinted from the *Studio*, November, 1888.

[5] From the account in the Norwich *Bulletin*.

[6] The address does not appear to have been published, but it has fortunately been preserved in manuscript among the Norton papers in the Houghton Library (Harvard College Library, Nor 5257.25F*). I owe the identification of this manuscript, the opportunity for my assistant to examine it in detail on an Interlibrary Loan, and permission to quote from it to the kindness of my friend William A. Jackson, Librarian of the Houghton Library. Special conveniences and courtesies for study of it in the Free Library of Philadelphia were graciously afforded by Dr. John H. Powell, Assistant Librarian in Charge of Research, and the staff of Pepper Hall.

[7] "An American Art-Scholar: Charles Eliot Norton," *Notes on Novelists*, New York: Charles Scribner's Sons, 1916, p. 422.

[8] Published in the *Studio* (New York), November, 1888. Reprints of it were made, one of which I still treasure.

CURATOR & LIBRARIAN
IN NORWICH

THE FANFARE OVER, my own job began — that of finding actual, practical ways of making the Museum do its work, of seeing that it was used and became an educational agent. At the same time, I was also responsible for administering and building up the Library.

Although there was a teacher of drawing in the Academy, the Curator of the Museum was the one who instructed the Seniors one hour a week in the history of art — architecture in the fall term, sculpture in the winter term, painting in the spring. A part of this teaching was done in the galleries of the Museum; some of it in a classroom with Museum photographs as illustrative material — for although, while I was at the Academy, the stereopticon was used to illustrate a few of the big evening lectures in the lecture hall, nothing of the sort was available for classroom use. Fortunately the classes were still small, perhaps ten or fifteen, so that the excellent photographs which formed an important part of the collection could be passed around for individual scrutiny.

A special attempt to connect the Museum and what it had to teach with the work of the Academy was the presentation in June, 1891, of seven tableaux from Book I of the *Iliad*. Dr. Keep selected the scenes to be shown, and the Curator with the students of the Normal and Art Schools designed and made the costumes (copied from the statues and Greek vases), made and hung garlands, and even constructed a Greek chair.[1] Help was given by the Boston Museum and the Director of the National Academy of Design in New York, and by the ladies in New Haven who had put on the production of *Antigone* that had inspired Dr. Keep to have something of the kind tried in Norwich. Dr. Keep gave the explanatory introduction to the performance, Mr. Griggs, the elocution teacher, was the reader before each scene, and the Academy and Art School students were the actors. The performance was a real success. The putting on of dramatic scenes and pageants is now an accepted part of educational procedure, but in the early nineties it was a comparatively new thing. Few schools had seen its educational possibilities, and probably no other secondary school had immediately at hand the museum and library facilities making possible the necessary research.

At the end of the first year, some attendance figures were published in an article by Edward Robinson entitled "The Cost of a Small Museum," which came out in the *Nation* for November 21, 1889. At that time the visitors' book showed more than ten thousand names, with an average weekly attendance of 283. The Academy scholars were not included in the list. The holiday attendance is striking — Thanksgiving Day, 800; Christmas, 932; New Year's, 732; Memorial Day (or Decoration Day, as we called it then), 850. A museum man then did not have many holidays — in those early days if the Museum was open, the Curator was there.

A careful record of attendance figures from 1888 to 1899 is still preserved among the Museum's records.

YEAR	DAYS OPEN	TOTAL ATTENDANCE
1888	19	2,762
1889	157	9,219
1890	154	7,478
1891	152	12,177
1892	152	7,641
1893	212	7,683
1894	200 (35 weeks)	8,416
Sept., 1894-Sept., 1895	310	11,079
1895-96	309	7,868
1896-97	308	6,075
1897-98	232	3,486
1898-99	312	5,119

For 1896-97 it was noted that no new exhibitions had been opened, and that Sachem Park was an increasing counter attraction.

The necessity for special exhibitions to induce people to keep coming to the Museum was something I soon realized, as the prestige of the grand opening and the novelty of the Museum began to wear off. So I arranged such exhibitions. The first was of Mr. Slater's paintings, chiefly of the Barbizon School, put on in January, 1890, which brought over three thousand visitors. I made a little six-page catalogue of the exhibition (my first special exhibition catalogue), titles and artists' names and dates only, printed in black and red. It shows, besides Rembrandt's "The Rabbi," three paintings by Corot, three by Dupré, two by Diaz, and one each of Millet, Troyon, Daubigny, Rousseau, Delacroix, Bertin, Courbet, Jacque, Passini, Raffaelli, Charles Chaplin, Courtois, and Knight. The paintings were shown again in January, 1891, with substantially the same catalogue. On June 11, 1894, they were hung again in the Museum, with a new catalogue, and remained there, with some changes, for several years. The paintings made a great impression on the students of the Art School and other visitors; they are often mentioned today by people recalling the Museum of that period.

From the Slater collections also, rugs, Beauvais tapestries, and Oriental embroideries and brocades were exhibited at various times.

Closely related to the Museum's own collection was an exhibition of colored photographs and casts "to illustrate the effect of color in Greek sculpture" (June, 1892). Exhibitions of this kind had been held in the Boston Museum and the Art Institute of Chicago following an article on the subject by Russell Sturgis in *Harper's Magazine* for September, 1890, and an article by Edward Robinson, "Did the Greeks Paint Their Sculpture?" had just come out in the *Century Magazine* (April, 1892).

Other exhibitions were "portraits of men and women connected with the early history of Norwich," an interesting group by well-known early painters, many Trumbulls among them (February, 1895); the work of Norwich silversmiths; a group of historical Norwich publications; and early printed children's books (June, 1899), mostly English, but some American. I must say that Norwich lived up to its reputation in producing old objects out of its collections.

An exhibition of bookbindings (December, 1894) displayed fine bindings lent by William Loring Andrews (who in The Grolier Club days was to become my friend), Mr. Slater, Elisha L. Palmer, the Columbia College Library, and Samuel P. Avery, with some contemporary commercial bindings lent by publishers. The catalogue was described in the *Library Journal*[2] in the following notice:

"Slater Memorial Museum. An Exhibition of Bookbindings. December, 1894. 24 p. A useful little pamphlet, describing the chief epochs and styles of binding, famous binders of past and present, and terms used in bookbinding; prepared as a guide to a collection of bindings exhibited in the museum. Contains a short list of 'Books and articles of reference to be found in the Peck Library.'"

A list in the Museum files indicates that twenty-seven exhibitions were held during my time, of many different sorts of material. In these years I was acquiring by personal experience a knowledge of what goes into special exhibitions — the first idea, the assembling, the installation and labeling, the making and printing of the catalogue, the handling of the publicity, the keeping of records, the careful and prompt return of

objects to the lenders, even sometimes the instructor's
or guide-lecturer's job of helping students to enjoy
and understand the exhibit. I was learning a lot about
the problems and routines involved in loan exhibitions.

The last two exhibitions listed before I left Norwich
suggest in a small way types of intermuseum co-
operation that were to be more fully experimented
with at a later time. On September 20, 1899, the Slater
Museum became a member of the Library Art Club,
and for some years thereafter received various exhibitions assembled and circulated by them. The library
world was a jump ahead of museums in attempting
what the American Federation of Arts was to do later.

In January, 1900, the Slater Museum was showing
an exhibition of material related to Cromwell, lent
by the City Library Association of Springfield, Massachusetts. This was one of the outgrowths of my association with the Springfield Library and John Cotton
Dana, for whom, as I shall tell in Chapter VIII, I had
lately brought together a collection of casts and photographs.

One often wonders what the people who come to
exhibitions in museums think of them. I once got a
chance to know what a man of wit thought of one of
ours. Among the special exhibitions I arranged was
one of chairs, to show their historical and artistic development — Byzantine to Chippendale — chosen from
the collection of George S. Palmer. When they were
being shown, Colonel Charles A. Converse, a prominent citizen of Norwich, came in to see them, and I

took him about and tried to answer his questions, his interest being largely in the values of such things. I told him as well as I could. The figures, though not so large as they would be nowadays, were impressive enough. Suddenly he lifted his hands to heaven, rolled up his eyes, and exclaimed, "Here speaks the comforter!" You will see his point when I tell you that Mr. Palmer made his money in a family firm which had a monopoly in the manufacture of comforters, or comfortables, for beds. It is pleasant to remember that the Art School is now housed in the Converse Art Building, erected in 1905 in accordance with the Colonel's bequest.

All sorts of people came to see the Museum, from many places. A quick glance at some of the old attendance books shows visitors from Canada, Mexico, Bermuda, England, Scotland, France, Germany, and Singapore, as well as from such far-flung cities of the United States as San Francisco, Minneapolis, Topeka, Chicago, Terre Haute, Toledo, Cleveland, Asheville, Houston, New Orleans, and San Mateo, Florida. A lot of distinguished people came too, for, as Mr. Robinson wrote me in 1892, "among the people whose good opinion is most worth having, it is always known as one of *the* museums of the country." At whatever hour these out-of-town visitors came, it was the custom to show them around, and this too fell to my lot. Sometimes the remarks some of these celebrities had to make were rather surprising. Once I took President Benjamin Harrison around, with his guard. He had nothing to say about the classical part of the collection, but when he came to Donatello's Saint John the Baptist, thin and gaunt, he broke his silence, asking me whether I considered it to be a good likeness. I don't remember what I replied, but I know he went on, "Have you here any portraits of the Jehovah?" That was a poser, coming from a President!

Meanwhile, Dr. Keep and the Academy authorities, in accord with President Gilman's closing admonition to "enlarge its facilities" and to "widen the opportunities to profit by" the Museum, had established in rapid succession a Normal School (1889), an Art School (1890), and a manual training department (January, 1891). Each of these opened new possibilities of use for the Museum.

Though the Art School and the Normal School were independent units, separate from the secondary school of the Free Academy and for older students, all three were closely affiliated with one another and with the Slater Museum, and hopes and designs for education through the use of the Museum naturally embraced them all. Thus the prospectus of the Art School for 1895-96 has this statement, doubtless written by Dr. Keep: "The connection of the Art School with the Free Academy, and with the Normal School and its schools of practice, enables it to bring the spirit and aims of the best art work in the country to bear upon children and young people at the very beginning of their course in drawing."

Through the Normal School, under the direction of Miss Ellor Carlisle, afterward, as Mrs. Ripley, Assistant Superintendent of Schools in Boston, were begun some experiments in the use of the Museum by public school classes. It will be remembered that the Academy, though a privately owned institution, was conceived in a spirit of close relationship to the public schools, so there was no such gap as would exist today between a private secondary school with its museum and the local public elementary schools. Nevertheless, in the nineties, museum visits by public school classes were a new field. Mrs. Ripley, full of ideas, has very kindly sent me some notes of what went on under her direction and permitted me to use them:

"In the early nineties a small group of the youngest children from the nearby public school was taken to the Museum. The story of the cast visited was told, and then, to avoid the scurry and scramble natural to such an excursion, the little first-graders were set to drawing what they saw. In view of their capacities, the straight lines and obvious angles of the Archaic were chosen as first objects. Some of the drawings were astonishing — striking in their expression and likeness to the original. After enough of sketching, there was more or less productive walk and pause through rooms of later periods. At one point an almost terrified hush enveloped the little ones when one small Negro boy, wide and white-eyed, pointed to a huge centaur and whispered, 'There is God!' But all were pleased to come again to the Museum. Later, grades above the first were brought to the Museum. In this manner, some of the children in Norwich had creative experience in relations between school and museum."

With the closing of the Normal School in 1896, this 63

early experiment in work with the public schools was temporarily abandoned. But the seed of the idea remained. In 1914, long after I left Norwich, Miss Faith R. Leavens, one of my former students at the Academy, organized talks and Museum visits for school children, first with volunteer workers and later with the help of Art School students — much to the pleasure of Mr. Slater, whose hopes and desires for the use of the Museum and the improvement of education in Norwich had always been comprehensive. Of course by this time instructor service and work with the public schools were well under way in many of the larger museums, but Miss Leavens' attempt seems to have been a recrudescence of Norwich's own experiments in this direction.

Another contact of some of the Norwich children with the Museum was the Saturday morning class for children conducted by the Art School. Begun in January, 1894, the class for the year 1894-95 numbered sixteen, and included children as young as five and six. A part of their program included sketching from the casts and stories about the casts. This class has continued without much interruption to the present day, including at present about sixty-five children — though not always with the same emphasis on use of the Museum.

In 1896-97 the Saturday morning class for children was taught by Miss Edith R. Abbot, an Art School student. In 1915, after ten years of successful teaching in the Art Department at Wellesley College under Miss Alice V. V. Brown, Miss Abbot consented to leave

64

her associate professorship there to try a year at the Metropolitan Museum, under my direction as Supervisor of Educational Work, as one of the two Museum instructors. She continued a much valued member of the educational staff until her retirement in 1944.

The Art School, opened in 1890, although not a large school, was an important institution. Two paragraphs in an early prospectus (1895-96) suggest how the school was intended to fit into the plan sketched out at the time of the Museum's opening.

"Like the Slater Museum, with which it stands in close relation, the Art School aims to promote the general advantage of the community. It offers to students exceptional advantages in the way of a thorough art education, and seeks to promote the application of art to industry.

"The studios of the school are in the Memorial building, five rooms being occupied by the various departments. The studios of the day classes, on the upper floors, communicate directly with the Museum, the varied collections of which are accessible daily and are constantly studied and used by the students."

The school laid special stress upon design and its application to industry and to the training of designers for textile and jewelry factories, in which Connecticut abounded, though, in effect, less use seems to have been made by local industries of locally trained designers than was hoped. Nevertheless, through the years, the school graduates have fitted into local industries in various ways; others have become teachers and museum workers. A scholarship was 65 available to the Art Students' League in New York and to the School of Drawing and Painting in Boston, and to these schools a number of the more talented and serious graduates went for advanced work. The Art School, too, usually had some evening classes, and townspeople studying for their own pleasure, without expectation of professional use, have always been a welcome part of the school.

A course in the history of art, or some part of it, was usually offered, and sometimes I taught this class — in 1891-92 the history of art, in the fall term of 1892 the history of sculpture, in 1898-99, Greek sculpture. I also gave individual lectures or series of lectures from time to time. The *Academy Journal* notes some of them — January 30, 1891, Assyrian, Egyptian, and Grecian art, especially architecture, for the evening art class; December, 1893, after I came back from the European trip described in Chapter VII, a lecture on "Impressions of the Art Galleries of the Vatican" and another on "The Museums of Athens." In 1898 I was giving a course in the history of art to the students of the Preparatory Department of the Art School, arranged to familiarize them with the contents of the Museum, and Ozias Dodge, then director of the school, supervised the sketching from the casts. When in July, 1895, a three weeks' summer school was held in the Academy, I was appointed to give lectures on the casts and on the paintings from Mr. Slater's collection then hanging in the Museum.

The first "Directress" of the Art School was Irene Weir, niece of the painter J. Alden Weir and of John F.

Weir of the Yale Art School. Alice V. V. Brown, connected with the school from the beginning, headed it with distinction from 1894 to 1897, when she went to Wellesley College to build up its department of art. She was succeeded by Ozias Dodge, who continued as Director until 1909. In 1912, Charlotte Fuller Eastman,[3] an Academy and Art School graduate and one of my pupils, became head of the school, after three years as its teacher of design; under her able guidance the school adapted itself to new conditions and the instruction of greatly increased numbers of Academy students.

Mrs. Eastman was one of the recipients of the scholarship offered to a Norwich student by the Boston Museum art school. The fact that as a young art student in Boston she immediately began earning her expenses, while testifying of course to her own special enterprise and ability, also indicates something about the caliber of the Norwich Art School and some of its gifted, eager students in the school's first decade.

Remembered almost with adoration by the students of those years is Miss Kate Morse, the teacher of design from 1892 to 1909. A radiant and lovely person, her lameness did not prevent her from being an effective teacher.

The prospectus of 1891-92 announced the sculptress Edith Woodman as the teacher of modeling and design, and again in the spring of 1899 she was conducting a class in modeling. In the interval she had become the wife of Bryson Burroughs, the painter. In 1898 Bryson Burroughs conducted a summer school with John H. Twachtman under the auspices of the Art

67

Students' League, and the following summer, the League having withdrawn from the project, he had his own school. In November, 1899, the Slater Memorial Museum exhibited the work of Edith Woodman Burroughs, Bryson Burroughs, Ozias Dodge, and Bela Lyon Pratt, with a small, four-page catalogue. My friendship with Edith and Bryson Burroughs began before their marriage and continued through their lifetime, giving me great pleasure. I remember Bernhard Berenson saying that when he came to America he always liked to visit in their home in Flushing, "where peace reigned."

A year after I went to the Metropolitan, Bryson Burroughs came there as Assistant Curator of Paintings under Roger Fry, the Curator; he himself became Curator in 1909. There he and I were associated in many activities, formal and informal.

Another person connected with the Art School who later came to the Metropolitan Museum was Miss Juliet W. Robinson. A student and assistant in the school, she too, like Miss Abbot, taught the Saturday morning class for children, in 1900-1901. In 1906 I asked her to come to the Metropolitan Museum to take charge of the work at the Information Desk, and just as in the Art School days her long, capacious pocket produced scissors, knife, and what not in the way of necessary tools, so now she was to have at her fingertips the many this's and that's of information needed by visitors to the Museum — ever lively, friendly, and helpful.

68   With the Art School students forming the nucleus

of an audience, it was possible to have from time to time lectures by art critics and artists to which the public was invited, as President Gilman had suggested at the inauguration of the building. I remember especially the lectures by Professor Morse on Japanese ceramics and Professor Niemeyer of Yale on painting. The formation of the Norwich Art Association in 1895, by students of the school, later joined by interested townspeople, helped bring in distinguished and able people as lecturers.

I sometimes think that if I had not fallen into a librarian's job, or a museum man's business, I should probably have become a printer. I had a special delight in things bibliographical, in types of various kinds, bindings, and design, and in Norwich I was allowed to make catalogues and other pieces of printing and to have them printed in the local job printer's office. Here, by the kindness of the Fates, a font of real Caslon type had been preserved from Colonial times, and used. You may be sure I used it too, in my humble efforts.

What I suppose was my first catalogue, however, the little catalogue of the Museum itself that came out early in 1889, was printed in Cambridge at the University Press. Dr. Keep wrote the introductory note.

Two or three years after the manual training department of the Academy was established in January, 1891, I persuaded Dr. Keep to include a course in printing, an unusual feature for a secondary school in those days. The catalogue of 1899-1900 reported: "The Printing Office [is] well equipped to do simple, ordinary work, and practically all the forms, blanks, letter-heads, programs and tickets, required in the various departments of the school, are done by student labor. . . . Four boys and three girls have learned to set type and the printing office is regarded by all as a very valuable feature of the school." As a matter of fact, since June, 1894, many of the forms had been printed by the Academy Press, including some of the small catalogues (leaflets of a few pages). By the date of the catalogue entry, the press was installed in the new manual training building opened September, 1895, and the young printers were about ready to attempt their first book — the *Journal* of Madam Sarah Knight[4] of Boston. This lively record of a horseback journey from Boston to New York and back in 1704 had an extra interest because Madam Knight was later a resident of Norwich, and was buried in New London. Donald G. Mitchell ("Ik Marvel") wrote the prefatory note. Although for nearly half a century he had been living at Edgewood, near New Haven, Norwich claimed Ik Marvel by right of birth; he had in fact lived for a time next door to what was later to become the site of the Academy. The introduction by W. R. Deane was a reprint from *Littell's Living Age* of June 26, 1858. The head- and tailpieces were largely the work of Miss Morse and the then Director of the Art School, Ozias Dodge, but the Curator of the Museum did one of them. The design for the cover came also from the Art School, and the binding was done in the Academy printing office. This was the third edition of 70 Madam Knight's *Journal,* and a very creditable edition it was, too. Daniel Coit Gilman, always interested in Academy doings, in acknowledging his copy said: "Aside from the intrinsic worth of this volume, it is to me a fine illustration of one phase of the Academy's activities. The arts of design, typography, and binding are well represented in this book."

Some time before this I had found one day in a cupboard in the Pastor's study of the old church a communion cup of silver, with wire handles, but as black as your hat. Cleaned, it allowed one to read the name of its maker, John Dixwell of Boston, and an engraved inscription which said, "The gift of Sarah Knight to the/Chh of Christ in Norwich/Ap^r 20, 1722." This I placed in a case in the Museum. Later, when the church needed money, George S. Palmer bought it and took it away. In time he sold it to Philip L. Spalding of Boston, another early collector of American silver, and at his death it was given to the Boston Museum and is now one of its treasures.

It must be remembered that all this time I was still a librarian as well as a museum curator. I worked closely with the teachers of the Academy and, with the funds available, added a valuable lot of books and magazines, laying of course a good deal of emphasis on art. Large additions in the field of art, with special reference to the Slater Museum, were made in the first year. In the Academy catalogue of 1889-90 the entire number of books in the Library was given as between six and seven thousand. A comparison of the Peck Library with other school libraries, published in the *Academy Journal* of March, 1892, showed it to be, with then nearly eight thousand volumes, by far the largest in the state, its nearest competitor reporting only two thousand volumes. The academical department of Phillips Andover had about three thousand volumes; Phillips Exeter 1,500. Few school libraries subscribed to periodicals, the largest number elsewhere being eleven; Peck at this time had forty-five. Only three other school libraries reported card catalogues. When I left Norwich in June, 1900, the Library contained, according to a note in the *Library Journal* of July, 1900[5] about twelve thousand volumes, sixty-five periodicals and newspapers on file, and an author and title catalogue. Books were issued to teachers and pupils of the Academy and beginning in January, 1893, to teachers of the public schools. The Library was open for general reference use every day from 2 to 5 p.m.

Today it is still one of the largest school libraries in the country, and in the field of art it ranks with college rather than secondary school libraries.

From 1895 to 1897 I had as my assistant in the Library Miss Winifred E. Howe, an Academy graduate. In 1910, after college and some years of teaching, she came at my request to the Metropolitan Museum. For a year, she assisted Miss Robinson at the Information Desk; then I took her into my office to work on publications. In her thirty years' service as Editor of Publications she set standards new in such matters in museums.

During these years I was participating in the American Library Association and the Connecticut Library

Association, and in March, 1899, was elected one of the vice-presidents of the latter. Librarians, you see, were already well organized, locally and nationally, owing in great part to Mr. Dewey's genius in this direction. Associations of museum workers came much later, and the Museum spirit was still to come.

NOTES

[1] I am indebted to Mrs. Ellor Carlisle Ripley, former head of the Normal School, for reminding me of these details. A program and newspaper clippings on file in the Slater Museum also refreshed my recollection of dates and other facts.

[2] Vol. 20, March, 1895, p. 105.

[3] I have Mrs. Eastman to thank for much skillful and sympathetic help given my assistant in bringing together some of the precise dates and details supplementing my own memories of my years in Norwich. Mrs. Ozias Dodge, now Curator of the Slater Memorial Museum, Miss Elizabeth E. Bean, Librarian of the Peck Library, Miss Margaret L. Triplett, Director of the Art School, and Mrs. Lawrence R. Browning, the present teacher of design, were also most generous with their interest and time at a particularly busy season.

[4] The Private Journal /of Sarah Kemble Knight/ Being the Record of a Journey /from Boston to New York/ in the year 1704/ [Seal] /Norwich, Connecticut/ The Academy Press/ MCMI.

[5] Vol. 25, p. 345.

NORWICHTOWN

WAYS AND PEOPLE

ALL OF MY OWN TIME in Norwich was spent in acquainting myself with its history and manners and customs. Even if I had not been naturally interested in such things, I believe I should have caught a liking for them from the old Norwichtown people, who had inherited a respect for them. The love of ancestral things, furniture, silver, etc., existed there to a marked degree; the houses were full of it. Stedman used to say that I should write down what I came to know about the town's history, people, and possessions, and that meant much to me, coming from one who had himself written so well about the old town.

I should explain, perhaps, the difference between "Norwich" and "Norwichtown." When the city was incorporated, the old town came to be called Norwichtown. In my day the old folks still called the city, or Norwich, "the Landing," because there the many ships had always docked.

Anyone who knows Miss Frances Manwaring Caulkins's *History of Norwich, Connecticut: From Its*   75

Possession by the Indians, to the Year 1866[1] would not
wonder at the effect of living in the old town on a boy
from, let us say, Boston, at his delight in what he saw
and heard, and what he learned. So many things she
talks about were still to be seen there, were still happening, not the Indian fights, to be sure, but all sorts
of other things which persisted, happily, through
habit. The town was purchased from the Indians June
6, 1659, by English colonists, who had come to Say-
brook first, but who left that place under the guidance
of the Reverend James Fitch and Major John Mason,
who happened to be friendly with the Mohegan Indians. I always liked the story of how this happened,
all gossip, I suppose, but possible. It was because the
maize planted as a crop, when it began to mature,
drew down crows and blackbirds in such numbers as
to blot out the light of the sun, and the crop was
destroyed. So some of these good Puritans determined
to leave the Sound, and the Saye and Sele Fort, and
to seek for a place where these marauders were not so
thick, and they came to the township of "Mohegan,"
or Norwich, as they afterwards called it, though just
why so named, nobody knows. I used to think that the
English name was given by someone who came from
that Norfolk city, a Leffingwell or a Backus, perhaps,
and when I was Librarian of the Academy Library, I
established a friendly relationship with its Lord
Mayor.

Norwich brings one close to the Indians, closer than
most towns do. The town was bought from the Mohe-
gans, and the relations between them and the early

settlers were friendly and constant. Their burial ground was respected, and when it was decided to erect a monument in honor of the great Chief Uncas, it was in the burial ground that it was placed. Before the monument was erected the graveyard was thick with Indian graves. A stone belonging to Samuel Uncas, a Sachem, was removed in my day to the Museum. The inscription, written by Dr. Elisha Tracy, a physician of the Revolutionary time, reads:

> For Beauty, wit, for Sterling sense,
> For temper mild, for Eliquence,
> For Courage Bold, for things wauregan,
> He was the Glory of Moheagon,
> Whose death has Caused great Lamentation,
> Both in ye English and ye Indian Nation.

I myself saw the last burial of a full-blooded Indian in that plot, one who had asked that he be wrapped, as he was, in the American flag.

According to Miss Caulkins, the cornerstone of the monument to Chief Uncas was laid in 1833 by President Andrew Jackson, with a good deal of fuss and feathers, but at that time no funds had been obtained for erecting the monument, and it was not until the Fourth of July, 1842, that the present granite shaft was actually raised, with only the one word, Uncas, on it.

Meanwhile, just a year before, a monument had been erected to Uncas's vanquished enemy, Miantonomo, the Narragansett chief, largely at the instigation of William C. Gilman, Daniel Coit Gilman's father. Long years before, a pile of stones had marked the traditional spot of Miantonomo's first capture and, according to local belief, also the place of his execution by Uncas. But the heap of stones, or cairn, and the two oak trees between which it stood had long since disappeared.[2] For identification of the spot, when the monument was to be set up, the party relied on the boyhood memory of N. L. Shipman, Esq., then an elderly gentleman, to whom everyone looked for historical facts. He was asked to lead the procession from the city to the field, out of town, where the ceremony was to be held. Here, at a pair of bars, he descended from his carryall, and walking into the five-acre lot, he stuck his cane down and said, "This is the spot," and the foundation for the monument was dug. Afterwards his son said to him, "Father, how did you know the exact spot where the Chief fell?" To which the wise old gentleman replied, "My son, that was no time for hesitation."

Bean Hill, a part of the original town, according to tradition was associated with the dish of baked beans, the Indians having shown the way to bake them in the Connecticut style, not the Boston beanpot kind, but baked in a milkpan, with nicely browned ones on top, much better than the soupy kind, if I may be allowed to judge. The Indians taught the settlers a lot about corn, too. On Bean Hill was located one of the early potteries in New England, making pots, mower's rings, to carry water on the arm, and penny banks. Thomas Harland, an English clockmaker, settled in Norwich in 1773 and taught all Connecticut to make good clocks with brass works. He also supervised the construction of Norwichtown's first fire engine. Grover Cleveland's grandfather, William Cleveland, was a silversmith here, and there were several others. Christopher Leffingwell set up a paper mill in 1766, and the printing of a newspaper began in 1773 — the *Norwich Packet*. Since then, Norwich has had many newspapers, weekly and daily. One, the morning *Bulletin,* begun in 1858, is still published daily. One of its early editors was Isaac H. Bromley. Another paper, a weekly, begun in 1852, the *Norwich Tribune,* had as its editor at one time our old friend Edmund C. Stedman, the poet.

One couldn't turn round without running up against interesting historical facts and names, as, for example:

Many Huntingtons, including Samuel, signer of the Declaration, President of the Continental Congress, and Governor of Connecticut, whose house attempted to copy Mount Vernon and was the most pretentious in the town; and Major General Jabez Huntington, who gave his fortune to Connecticut in the Revolution, even permitting the leaden weights by which his windows hung to be cast into bullets, and who was the father of three daughters and five sons, four of whom served with distinction in the Revolution.

Jonathan Trumbull of Lebanon, the Governor, who according to Miss Caulkins was the original "Brother Jonathan," a name given casually by George Washington when addressing him — "What does Brother Jonathan think?" he would say — which became the name used for all Americans, our sobriquet.

Benedict Arnold, who, as a young man, was a clerk

in Dr. Lathrop's drugstore, and a naughty one, too. He afterwards went to England, and then became a druggist on his own, in New Haven, and hung out his sign, which read: "B. ARNOLD, DRUGGIST,/ Book-Seller, &c./ FROM LONDON./ Sibi Totique."—a motto which gives food for thought, "for himself and for all."

I mentioned in an earlier chapter how I found the silver communion cup given by Madam Sarah Knight to the old church. In the Pastor's study I found also the church's pewter communion tankard and cups, used before silver began to be used—long before Madam Knight gave the cup; these I also took to the Museum. In a room in the steeple of the church, to which the Pastor's library had been banished years before, I came upon a rare lot of early printed books of sermons and the theology of the day, written by the ministers of churches all round about and all printed in Norwich or nearby places; when the church needed money to reshingle the roof I arranged for their sale to Lathrop Harper in New York, who tells me that many of them went to the American Antiquarian Society in Worcester. This was a case when Colonial theology was very useful and whatever worth it had was appreciated indeed.

Such names and things as these were of consuming interest and led me to lay in knowledge which was of the greatest use to an archaeologist or historically minded person, material of value to me all my life in museums and libraries.

It should not be forgotten that these were the days of our first collectors of Americana, men like Eugene

Bolles of Boston, George Palmer of New London, Dwight Blaney of Boston, Harry H. Flagler of New York, and several others, and my acquaintance with them all was due to what I knew and could tell about the treasures of Norwich. Some of the best furniture in The Metropolitan Museum of Art, bought from George Palmer, came from Norwichtown and Yantic. But of these men I will speak further when I come to the chapter on the Metropolitan Museum and what it did with their help for the arts and crafts of this country.

One of my friends in Norwichtown was Miss Mary E. Perkins, whose interest in the place led her to the writing of a book on the old houses,[3] architectural, historical, and biographical; and there were ways in which I could and did help her, by drawing maps and plans, and by acting as agent for the publication. The book, with its many pictures, was a success, and takes its place alongside Miss Caulkins's *History*, supplementing it with its different kind of information. A second volume was planned, but, unfortunately, was not finished.

Norwich, the city, in my day was celebrated for its houses, gardens, hothouses, and food. It had a large number of millionaires among its mill owners, folk who liked such things. Among those who were distinguished and whose acquaintance was beneficial to a young man were two whose friendship I especially valued. One was David Ames Wells, writer on political economy, apostle of free trade, member of the Cobden Club, and Representative in Congress for Connecticut. He drove out every fair afternoon in a waggon, behind a pedigreed Arab stallion, one of a group of three which General Grant had received as a gift from the Khedive of Egypt and which he gave to Mr. Wells; and he often took me with him. He being scientifically minded had small use for museums of art, but what he told me about rocks, trees, and such-like things was grist to my mill of education. His library was given by his son to the Springfield Library while John Cotton Dana was its librarian. His friend Senator Lafayette S. Foster, elected President pro tempore of the Senate in March, 1865, upon the death of President Lincoln became, by virtue of his office, nominal Vice-President of the United States. Senator Foster's widow lived near the Slater Museum, and was most friendly in her notice of the cub curator.

Mrs. Foster drove out in a dogcart with a tiger up behind, and she used to come to meals in black silk gloves. One day at a luncheon to which I was invited ice cream was served, and Professor Hutchison, who was cheerfulness itself, said: "Madam Foster, the man who invented ice cream should have been canonized," but Mr. Wells, not so polite, and with his mouth full, said: "He should have been damned, Madam."

I went one day with Mr. Wells behind his Arab stallion to Yantic, to a real old-fashioned vendu, or auction, in the Backus House, after the death of the last one of a family that settled Norwich and, later, Ohio. It was known how full the house was of old things, and great crowds of dealers came to the barbecue, and then to bid. I swept up a mass of papers, thrown out by the executors, and having put them in a barrel and two soapboxes, asked the auctioneer to put them up for sale. This he did, and I got the lot for a dollar. Among the treasure trove were many rare books, pamphlets, and maps, the Battles of Concord and Lexington engravings by Doolittle in color, and other engravings of real value and rarity. Best of all was a diary written by a Backus boy, Elijah, Jr., when a Senior at Yale in 1777, a priceless piece of Yale memorabilia in which the chap gave a daily record of his classes and teachers, rumors of troop movements and fighting, and, later, the progress of an epidemic of smallpox in New Haven which disrupted the college and sent him home, and then to the Pest House for inoculation.[4]

The critic may say, after reading this chapter, what has all this to do with education for museum work? But if he had known Norwichtown in the days I have talked about, its people and its houses, he would have seen that they were reminiscent of Colonial days and history and devoted to them. Norwichtown gave me an interest in American history, architecture, arts and crafts, all of which, as I said before, were exemplified there, and this interest stood me in good stead; for instance, it led me to recommendations made to Mr. de Forest at the time of the Hudson-Fulton celebration in 1909, when the Curator of Paintings had advised a showing of Dutch paintings. I said to Mr. de Forest, who was then Secretary of the Metropolitan Museum, that it seemed to me a museum which showed Greek, Roman, Egyptian, Chinese, and other Eastern things surely ought to show to its public the things America had accomplished. He saw the point, and appreciated the soundness of the argument, and so to the exhibition of Dutch paintings representing Hudson's period was added an exhibition of American furniture, silver, pottery, etc., representing Fulton's period, which I brought together, with the help of Miss Florence Levy, borrowed from my collector friends, Palmer, Bolles, Blaney, Halsey, Flagler, and others. This was the first time American "antiques" were ever shown in New York, and they made a great hit, with public and dealer alike. The Hudson-Fulton effort resulted eventually in the American Wing. But of that I shall speak later.

It is interesting to reflect that at the opening of the Slater Museum even a person like President Gilman, familiar with Norwich and quick to see the possible influence of a museum on the arts and crafts of an industrial city, did not mention the examples of American arts and crafts of an earlier period of which the town was so full. Still less did Mr. Norton have anything good to say about American art. Bewailing the lack of beauty and taste in American houses *(sic!)*, furniture, and articles of daily use, he seemed unaware that a native tradition existed, with surviving examples all around him. The collectors, as I have said, had begun to be aware of these things, but it was to be many years yet before early American decorative arts would come into general acceptance and public acclaim.

NOTES

[1] The first edition of this book was published in Norwich by Thomas Robinson in 1845, under the title, *History of Norwich, Connecticut, from Its Settlement in 1660, to January 1845;* the author was named on the title-page as "Miss F. M. Caulkins." A second, greatly expanded, edition, printed in Hartford, was "published by the author" in 1866. The third edition, using sheets from the edition of 1866, with an added "Brief Sketch of the Life of the Author" and an "Appendix, Containing Notes and Sketches continuing the History to the Close of the Year 1873," and with some changes in plates, was "published by the friends of the author" in 1874. I have used both the second and the third edition in preparing my text.

[2] Frances Manwaring Caulkins, *History of Norwich, Connecticut . . . ,* Norwich, 1874, pp. 37-38, 585-586.

[3] Mary E. Perkins, *Old Houses of the Antient Town of Norwich, 1660-1800.* Norwich, Conn., 1895.

[4] Ellen D. Larned, "Yale Boys of the Last Century," *Connecticut Quarterly,* vol. 1, October-December, 1895, pp. 355-361.

Norwichtown Ways and People

85

EUROPEAN NOTEBOOK

AFTER TWO OR THREE YEARS in the Slater Museum I realized how necessary a trip abroad was, if I was to go on as a museum worker. At the beginning of 1893 I was given the rest of that school year off by my Trustees for travel in Europe, and Mr. Slater generously gave me the money to cover my expenses. Mr. Robinson, President Gilman, and others helped me with letters of introduction and suggestions of people to see.

Having great interest in the Byzantine architecture, I planned to visit first the countries where it could be seen, and then to follow in other countries the development of later styles of building. I sailed for Naples and went from there directly to Palermo, where I saw my first Byzantine architecture with delight — the Capella Palatina and the great church of Monreale, outside the town, both certainly very beautiful and the most perfect introduction to the subject. I saw also the Greek temples at Girgenti and Syracuse; I looked up at Etna, from Catania and, after I sailed for Athens, on the ship, looking back, until she disappeared over the horizon.

The arrival at Piraeus in the early morning was dramatic, and the first sight of Athens was thrilling — 87 like finding something you had always been looking for. I had plenty of notes to people here, all useful, and the American School took me in as its guest, Professor Wheeler, the Director, being most kind. It was here that I first met Albert Lythgoe, who was taking the course in Greek archaeology before he became interested in Egyptian art. I also met Richard Norton, Charles Eliot Norton's son, and "Dodo," E. F. Benson, the son of the English Archbishop and brother of A. C. Benson, of Magdalene College, Cambridge, of *College Window* fame.

Dodo's lack of knowledge about some things was extensive. He was told off to make an address when members of the English and German Schools visited the American School, and he spoke on "Physicians in Greece." He took occasion to refer to the American medicine men, and he said, "In America, medicine men allow themselves to be bitten by snakes in order to work certain cures." Sitting next to Richard Norton, I asked him if his doctor did that in Cambridge.

I had letters to Dr. Dörpfeld, the great Athenian scholar, and he courteously allowed me to attend his lectures on the topography of the Acropolis. I also went to lectures by Dr. Gardner in the new Acropolis Museum on the recently discovered Acropolis sculptures. The Norwich casts of Greek sculpture now began to have real meaning, and I must say a new beauty.

From Athens I went to Constantinople. I thought I was not unprepared for the beauty of the church of Santa Sophia, now a mosque, but it bowled me over, even if Professor Whittemore had not yet got busy with cleaning the mosaics. After the book on Santa Sophia by Lethaby and Swainson was published in 1894, I read it to my classes in Norwich with great delight. I also gave a series of evening lectures on Santa Sophia to the art students. My enthusiasm must have communicated itself to some of my listeners, for several of them have kindly mentioned the course in recent days as something vividly remembered from their art-student years.

I made a careful study of the mosque Kahrieh Jami, called the mosaic mosque. Originally the church of a monastery, it had mosaics then being uncovered which might have been made after designs by Giotto. H. G. Dwight says in his great book on Constantinople, "If the Renaissance was a reflowering, it was of a plant that had silently grown in another soil. And Kahrieh Jami is the last flower of that plant in its own Byzantine ground."[1]

The mosques, with their minarets, fountains, and gardens, the sea and the country round about, the people — everything Turkish — were a delight. I was sorry, when the time came, to go back to the more prosaic Athens.

From Athens I traveled on to Italy and visited the Italian cities, going north; then to Switzerland, Germany, Belgium, France, England; and from there home, in time to take up my work in Norwich with the opening of the fall term. Wherever I went, though not forgetful of the libraries, my chief business was visiting the museums, where I made sketches and notes on what I saw and heard. The museum on the Acropolis at

Athens had been lately built to contain the small painted *Tantefiguren,* which had recently been found and were exciting great interest. The city's own museum had been rearranged, and the sculptures at Olympia were but recently set up. The museum at Constantinople was not yet opened when I was there, but the Director, Hamdi Bey, to whom I had letters from Dr. Gilman and Mr. Robinson, was so good as to let me see the recently found Sidonian sarcophagi, on which at that time the color was still fresh. I was allowed to have photographs of the Alexander sarcophagus, which I afterwards gave to Helbig of the German School in Rome and to Professor Curtius, the historian of Greece, in Berlin. In all these places I spent my days in museums and churches, and filled my notebook with sketches and notes, laying my emphasis on the methods of exhibition and on all the details connected with the display and presentation of the collections.

The things which I saw in these museums that interested me particularly, as the "museum man," of course, not as the student of art, were many — how their public was treated; what privileges were given, and what was done for their comfort; what catalogues were published; how objects were labeled; what the printing was like; how the objects were shown and the little tricks of display to enhance the effect; what colors were used. Smoking rooms and lounges were unknown until long afterwards, but I was curious about the styles for chairs and benches, frames, bulletin boards, and pedestals. Wall coverings for galleries where paintings were shown were usually of rich materials, and in shades of red. All these things, like the galleries themselves, were copies of the styles set in palaces.

In such matters, I found that certain museums studied their problems and did the things they turned their attention to very well. All, I afterwards learned, were being inspired by men like Bode and what resulted in his "period arrangement" in the Berlin Museum, and by those who were to invent the so-called "room arrangement" so beautifully carried out in Zurich, Nuremberg, and Munich, to whom the whole museum world is under obligation. The Germans gave very real attention to the problems of arrangement, display, and management of museums of every kind. This visit opened my eyes, of course, to many things and, with later visits in after years, I was fortunate enough to see what was really a development of what we may call the modern museum idea, which I believe had its inception in Napoleon's conquests and in the study of art and archaeology which followed. I was greatly impressed by what I saw now and on later visits in the German and Swiss cities, and I learned lessons I have never forgotten. The National Museum of Belgium in Brussels had some tricks of display worth remembering, especially for textiles, and so had the Musée Galliéra in Paris. But all of these inventions, it will be understood, were developed after the South Kensington Museum had done its great part in teaching methods of display, which in their day were way ahead of such efforts in other countries.

Curiously enough, few of the museums which I visited on my first trip, or later, were noteworthy for what is now called "functional" architecture, most of them being old palaces or monasteries, or what might be called "museum architecture," the Vatican-Louvre sort of thing, or developed from those buildings. The little Acropolis museum showed signs of thought having been expended on it; the Munich National Museum, the museums of Hesse-Darmstadt and Zurich, and the Musée Galliéra, all gave the impression of logical, thoughtful development in their buildings — thoughtful for their date. Before the time when these museums were built, it would seem that the only problem studied by builders of museums was the one of light for pictures and how best to get it in galleries.

My notebooks from this trip were a source of helpfulness to me in times of need; and in all the museums with which I was connected you may find furniture and gadgets copied from my drawings of such things in this and that European museum — benches and bulletin boards in New York like those in the Victoria and Albert Museum, photograph and textile cases in Springfield and New York like those in Brussels, frames and label holders like those in various places. These notebooks served me well, but were finally lost in the great New England hurricane of 1938. However, there appears to be a copy in the Slater Museum, which begins with Naples and goes on through Pompeii, Palermo, Athens, Constantinople, Rome, Orvieto, Florence, and Venice, ending with Munich, Dresden, and Berlin. It is the notebook, not of an art student, but of a student of museum administration, for it treats of such matters as admission fee, presence or absence of turnstile, catalogue, building, walls, lighting, furniture, pedestals, labels, guards, as well as the nature and quality of the collections.

Years later, remembering my indebtedness to others, I had a pamphlet printed in the Metropolitan Museum[2] with drawings of everything, frames, pedestals, gadgets, etc., made and used in the Metropolitan Museum, on the model of the South Kensington book of a similar kind.

Doubtless all the things that I learned with such pleasure in Europe, other museum people also learned, even if they did not emulate them. But this is *my* education I am talking about, not theirs, and education, after all, is just learning what you did not know before.

NOTES

[1] *Constantinople: Settings and Traits,* New York: Harper & Brothers, 1926, p. 106.

[2] *Drawings and Measurements of Furniture Used by the Museum,* New York, 1923. Reprinted in 1930 in expanded form as *Furniture, with Drawings and Measurements, and Various Devices Used by the Museum.*

COLLECTIONS

OF CASTS

WHAT WITH THE normal work of the Library and
Museum, the classes of Academy boys and girls, and
lectures given from time to time to the Art School
students, the Curator kept busy indeed, but he never
forgot, one might say he was not allowed to forget,
another part of his job as prescribed by Mr. Slater, to
help form collections of reproductions for other schools
and towns that might want them. This involved trips to
other cities and meeting new people; it helped to make
life agreeable and varied.

Like so many other uses of the Slater Museum, this
one, too, was foreshadowed in one of President Gilman's addresses — in this case the early address at the
dedication of the building in November, 1886. After
pointing out the example of South Kensington and
commenting on the value of reproductions for the
ordinary observer he continued: "Such museums [i.e.,
of reproductions] have already been begun in several
American cities. It will not be best to copy any one of
them, but rather to give to the Academy Museum a   95

character of its own, so choice and so instructive that the virtuosos from other places will come here to study it."

The desire of Mr. Slater to encourage and assist in the establishment of other museums was very explicitly stated by Edward Robinson in "The Cost of a Small Museum,"[1] which I mentioned in an earlier chapter — indeed, this is plainly the purpose of the article. It emphasized the importance of even a small city's having "its gallery of reproductions as well as its public library — a gallery in which children could grow up familiar with the noblest productions of Greece and Italy, in which the laborer could pass some of his holiday hours, and in which the mechanic could find the stimulus to make his own work beautiful as well as good." To show that the cost of such a collection was within reach of many cities, an analysis of the expense of assembling the Slater Museum was given; the article pointed out also that economy had not been a consideration in the execution of the Slater Museum.

As the assembling of collections of casts was an important chapter in the history of American museums, these figures may be interesting to repeat here: gross cost, excluding the building, $27,112.97; casts, including packing and transportation, $13,968.68; plaster-work, $1,626.75; carpentry (including a number of changes in the hall, which had not been built for a museum), $4,690; photographs, $800; electrotype coins, $750; balance, draperies and upholstery, photograph frames, designers' commission, and petty expenses.

One of the earliest of my associations in this sort of

96

work was with Mrs. Gustav Radeke in the selection of casts and photographs for the Rhode Island School of Design in Providence. Mrs. Radeke was the President of the School and was active also, at a later date, in the Federation of Arts and the Museums Association. Working with her was always a delightful experience. I remember being greatly impressed by the esteem shown for her, when I spoke at the Memorial Meeting for her in Providence in 1931. Her work and her plans were the agencies that made the Rhode Island School and Museum what they are today, among the best of their kind.

In 1891, the Trustees of The Metropolitan Museum of Art appointed a Special Committee on Casts to consider additions to the collection of casts then held — the Willard collection of architectural casts (bequest of 1883; casts first exhibited in 1889) and the sculptural casts secured from the gift of $10,000 by Henry G. Marquand in 1886. The declared purpose of the Committee, of which Mr. Marquand was chairman and Robert W. de Forest the active and much-interested vice-chairman, was "to obtain a complete collection of casts, historically arranged, so as to illustrate the progress and development of plastic art in all epochs, and mainly in those which have influenced our own civilization."[2] To this end it was hoped to raise $60,000 by subscription.

Edward Robinson, who had written a catalogue of the casts in the Boston Museum based on the Friederichs-Wolters catalogue of the Berlin Museum, brought together, with assistance from Professors Allan Marquand and A. L. Frothingham, Jr., of Princeton, *Tentative Lists of Objects Desirable for a Collection of Casts*, which included practically all the casts available at that time, with the cast makers' names, the prices, and the locations of the originals; it was printed for the Committee in June, 1891.

On Saturday, May 2, of that year the Special Committee and a number of other guests came to Norwich at Mr. Slater's invitation to study the installation in the Slater Museum. They left New York on the ten o'clock train in a special drawing-room car provided by Mr. Slater, who entertained them at dinner in his home, after they had visited the Museum and the town. Those attending from the Committee were Mr. de Forest, Edward D. Adams, Howard Mansfield, George F. Baker, Professor Allan Marquand, A. C. Merriam, F. D. Millet, F. W. Rhinelander, Augustus Saint-Gaudens, Professor William R. Ware, and Stanford White. The other guests, several of whom had declined the invitation to the formal opening of the Museum, were Andrew Carnegie, F. F. Thompson, E. L. Godkin, William E. Dodge, C. C. Beaman, Charles Stuart Smith, Brayton Ives, T. B. Clarke, R. W. Gilder, S. P. Avery, W. L. Andrews, and Theodore Weston.

The visit received a good deal of publicity, both in New York and New England. The New York papers not only gave considerable space to the plans of the Metropolitan, the composition of the Special Committee, the publication of the *Tentative Lists,* but also carried good descriptions of the Slater Museum, "said to be the finest one of the kind in the country." Of course they

maintained the prestige of the metropolis by emphasiz-
ing the great size of its projected collection. As the
Tribune said with guarded dignity: "The trustees of
the Metropolitan Museum of Art contemplate, as a
matter of course, the purchase of a much larger collection. Their visit, however, to Norwich was full of instruction."

The New England papers, naturally, gloated. "Connecticut," said the *Hartford Post,* "has been able to
furnish many useful and delightful things to a waiting
and wondering world, from buttons and clocks to
statesmen in every national crisis, but it has not been
dreamed that this state would be resorted to by the
trustees of the Metropolitan Art Museum of New York
for artistic information. Yet so it is."

The *Springfield Republican* commented: "One of
the most interesting and amusing of trips was that taken
by a New York committee in the interest of the Metropolitan Museum of Art to Norwich, Ct., Saturday. It
was interesting because taken in behalf of what will be
eventually the greatest institution of art in the United
States; and amusing when one reflects that such an institution is so behindhand that it goes to a rural town
like Norwich to find what it ought to do in the way of
buying and arranging casts. The Slater collection of
casts of ancient sculpture, now placed in the Slater
memorial at Norwich, has been excellently chosen, and
is artistically displayed by Edward Robinson of Boston,
one of the most thorough students and connoisseurs in
the world. It was well for the New Yorkers to learn of
him."

99

The little school paper, the *Academy Journal,* also reported the visit, gleefully insisting that the august visitors from New York spent a good bit of time at the windows of the Museum, overlooking the baseball game in progress on the school field.

Mr. Robinson, still in the Boston Museum, acted as purchasing agent for the big collection. He was assisted in Rome by Mrs. Elihu Vedder, wife of the artist, and by two or three agents in other European cities.

In November, 1893, the Committee on Arrangement of the Metropolitan Museum Trustees informed the Special Cast Committee that the ground floor of the new North Wing (Wing C) was to be allotted to the sculptural casts — the new collection and the Marquand collection combined. I was interviewed by Mr. de Forest, having been recommended by Mr. Robinson as the person to arrange the objects according to countries and schools. Mr. de Forest engaged me, and I fell to work with my plans, which were submitted from time to time to Mr. Robinson for his approval. I went frequently to Manchester, near Boston, where he had his summer house, and where, so to say, he edited my ideas. The job was a big one, and while no other collection even in Germany was so all-embracing, there was no hope of making it as effective in display as the Norwich one was. However, the work was finished in 1894, the North Wing, as it was then called, being opened with special ceremonies on November 5, 1894.

I had little to do with the setting up of the casts; that was left to General Cesnola's Curator of Casts, Dr. John Alsop Paine, who followed my drawings in the classification and arrangement. This was my first official connection with the Metropolitan Museum.

The group of Renaissance casts is still on exhibition, but much of the collection has been put in storage, crowded out by originals of their periods.

In Buffalo, in 1894, the Honorable James M. Smith made a gift of $5,000 to the Buffalo Fine Arts Academy, then housed in the Buffalo Library building. Half of this sum was expended on repair and alterations in the Academy gallery. In 1897 I was asked to select, purchase, and arrange casts with the remaining $2,500. This I did, and the gallery was opened January 14, 1899, with some thirty casts of Greek and Roman sculpture and sixteen photographs of Greek architecture. I spoke at the exercises and so did Melvil Dewey, then Secretary of the University of the State of New York, as well as Librarian of the State Library. He emphasized, as of course he would, the museum and the library as educational forces, and the importance of their working together to this end.

The *Illustrated Buffalo Express* for January 15, 1899, carried quite an account of the collection and exercises, with a picture of the casts being set up by the Italian workmen.

In 1905 the Albright Art Gallery of the Buffalo Academy was opened, with the casts in a new installation, but at present many of them are on loan to the Art School and the University of Buffalo.[3]

In 1898 and 1899 began my association with John Cotton Dana, newly arrived in Springfield as Librarian of the City Library Association, which became a friendship that lasted for the rest of his life and gave us both many amusing and lively hours; it was also an education for me in public relationships, of which he was a master.

Dana, born in Woodstock, Vermont, was attached to the Survey of Colorado, and in 1889 was made Librarian of the Denver Public Library, which under his management became noteworthy for the things done there. Dana was a person of many inventions and great enthusiasms, and he made himself distinguished in the profession. Indeed he was made President of the American Library Association, which Dewey had started, and served with great success. When the public library of Springfield, Massachusetts, needed a librarian, he was asked to go back to New England, and did. Here he applied all his abilities to his work and, again, helped to make the Springfield library known to librarians as a unique institution. He observed what had happened in Norwich, and conceived the idea of creating a small museum of reproductions, in association with the library.

Under a discretionary power, the Trustees of the Estate of Horace Smith gave funds for the purchase of casts, and books and photographs to supplement them, and for a proper installation in the gallery set aside for the collection in the Fine Arts Building. The Curator of the Norwich Museum, under Edward Robinson's direction, was employed to select and arrange the collection. Great care was taken with all the details of installation. The settees, the swinging photograph frames, and the photograph storage cases were designed by the young Curator who had come back from Europe with a full notebook, and much attention was paid to clear and attractive labeling, one of John Dana's pet ideas. The installation was one of real beauty.

The collection contained thirty-seven casts of Greek sculpture and thirty-six of Renaissance, six hundred photographs, and over a hundred books kept in the same room as the casts for easy reference use there.

Dana, as always, was full of schemes for making his library and museum useful. In this matter we saw eye to eye, even though in later years, when he was in Newark and I in the Metropolitan Museum, the methods by which we tried to work out this principle differed somewhat because of the different material and trustees we had to work with.

One of his ideas of making the collection useful to school children was the printing of a little pamphlet on Greek mythology, which was called "Stories of the Greek Sculptures," written by Edith Souther Tufts, then of the Norwich Free Academy and later Registrar of Wellesley College. This little sixteen-page pamphlet, still in circulation in Springfield, is a model of its kind. It pleased me greatly, because when I was a boy in the Latin School in Boston, we pupils were made to study Greek and Roman mythology, an important part of our education.

Lectures were given under the auspices of the Library Association to encourage attendance and understanding of the new collection. I gave four weekly lectures on Greek and Renaissance sculpture in November and December, following the opening in June,

1899. Talks were given by the Supervisor of Drawing in Springfield to various groups, including students of Greek history from the high school. A class of art students made visits to the museum and groups came to draw from the casts. A special invitation to street railway men to visit the museum — a characteristic Dana touch — brought out 150.[4]

A second pamphlet was designed not so much for the museum user as, having Mr. Slater's purpose in mind, for the prospective museum maker. *The Horace Smith Collection of Casts of Greek and Renaissance Sculpture: A Brief Statement of the Cost and Manner of Its Installation,* by Henry Watson Kent, published in January, 1900, had as its purpose to give an idea of the cost of the collection and "to answer some of the numerous questions that arise in the minds of those who are desirous of making similar collections." A list of some of the topics taken up gives an idea of the scope of the pamphlet: the room described; color of walls; manner of selection of casts; dealers and prices of casts; how the casts were set up; care of casts; spraying and hardening; the pedestals; books to accompany the collection; photographs and their manner of storage; the labels; seats and other furniture. At the end of the pamphlet is a closely itemized account of the cost of the collection and installation, totaling $8,557.28, and a list of the casts, with the place from which each was secured, and its price. The cost of the casts themselves, with packing and freight, was $4,054.83, the setting up, $414.90, treatment by Von Dechend process, a Berlin Museum machine for the hardening and cleaning of the casts, $342.12; the photographs and prints, $188.19, with mounting, mats, and frames adding $285.34; the books, $540.00. Woodwork (screens, pedestals, etc.), painting, and burlap for screens accounted for $1,-090.43; electric lighting for $136.29; furniture (which included book stands; photograph racks, cases, and a swinging frame; a table and a desk; and five settees) came to $740.25. Edward Robinson and H. W. Kent (together) received $500. Printing (labels and lists) and label holders cost $69.95. Various small items made up the remaining $194.98.

When the Special Cast Committee from the Metropolitan Museum came to Norwich, Mr. Andrew Carnegie, as I have said, came too, having expressed the desire to do so. I was delegated to take him about, and show him the sights. He didn't seem greatly interested, except in the electrotype copies of Greek coins, made by Ready of the British Museum. He asked what they were for, and I explained to him they were used in the teaching of Greek history and it was found that the boys had a liking for them. To which he replied, "You tell the boys to look after that little coin called the dime, and then these things will look after themselves."

I thought he was not interested in what Mr. Slater had done for Norwich or in the casts themselves, but afterward he gave money for a large collection of casts to the Carnegie Institute in Pittsburgh, and asked me to help in its formation. John W. Beatty was then the Director of the Department of Fine Arts there, and I worked with him from 1904 to 1906 in assembling the collection.

When the collection was opened in April, 1907, there were thirty-six architectural casts in the main display, including a splendid replica of the porch of the Romanesque church in Saint Gilles. A supplementary study collection of over a hundred pieces was in hand for later installation. The sculptural casts at the time of the opening numbered sixty-nine — four Egyptian, three Chaldean and Assyrian, three Persian, and fifty-nine Greek and Roman. The architectural casts on display now number 145; of sculpture, 84. No figures were published of the cost of the Pittsburgh collection, but because of the number of large architectural pieces, it considerably exceeded that of the Slater Museum.

While this collection was being brought together I was in New York, at The Grolier Club and then at the Metropolitan, but that the Norwich tradition was still fertile is suggested by a statement about the collection in the *Eleventh and Twelfth Annual Reports of the Director of Fine Arts, for the Years ending March 31, 1907, and March 31, 1908:*

"Briefly stated, the dominant purpose kept steadfastly in mind in forming the collections of casts of architecture and of sculpture has been to inspire in the mind of the visitor a love of the beautiful rather than to convey exclusively archaeological information. The definite aim was to create by the supreme dignity of the groups an inspiring and uplifting sense of the beauty of art as represented by these masterpieces of all time. The average visitor may forget the historical data, but an enduring impression of beauty will remain."

106   This collection exists today in substantially the same

installation, with an attractive spaciousness and dignity.[5]

These five — Providence, New York, Buffalo, Springfield, and Pittsburgh — were the main collections with which I helped under the impetus of the Slater Museum. But in estimating the Museum's influence we must remember that it was a model which many distinguished visitors came to inspect, and it doubtless had an effect on collections with which the Curator had no direct contact. For example, Miss Elizabeth Blanchard, Principal of Mount Holyoke Seminary, with Miss Anna C. Edwards, its Associate Principal, came to Norwich to visit the Museum. Mount Holyoke had had a course in the history of art as a regular part of its curriculum since 1878, close on the heels of Harvard in this then unusual inclusion, and Miss Blanchard was its teacher. It had had its art gallery (on the third floor of a laboratory and recitation building) since 1876, and was heading toward the opening of Dwight Memorial Art Building in 1901.[6] That there were other such visitors is plain from a statement of Dr. Keep's to the Connecticut Library Association, meeting in the Slater Memorial Museum on October 13, 1892, scarcely four years after the Museum's opening. "Since the establishment of the museum," he said, "many of the colleges of the country have taken steps towards forming similar ones. The influence of the museum, both in and out of Norwich, is far beyond what was expected at first, and the number of out-of-town visitors increases every year."[7]

Again, at the Fortieth Anniversary of the Academy, 107

in 1896, Dr. Keep reported: "The creation of our museum was an event of much significance for the study of art in America. It stood at that time almost alone. Since then it has served as the model for a considerable number of similar collections, and it has been so thoroughly described and so much visited that the formation of a new collection is hardly ever undertaken without careful examination of our own."

The Springfield pamphlet of 1900 mentioned that in the preceding ten years collections of casts had been made "in New York, Chicago, Providence, Buffalo, Worcester, Portland, Princeton University, Cornell University, and other places," and it is probable that most of these had sent some representative to visit the Norwich museum.

Help was given, too, to many libraries in the purchase from European photographers of photographs of art and architecture of all periods, especially those of France, including the carbon prints of Ad. Braun, then celebrated.

To young museum people who have grown up with the present opulence of museum collections, the early emphasis on reproductions is no doubt astonishing. And indeed, when we turn back to a statement made in 1885 by Pierre LeBrun, the architect, who was assembling the Willard collection of architectural casts for the Metropolitan Museum, we are startled by the wrongness of his prophecy of the future of American museums. "Collections of casts," he wrote in his report, "are springing up in all the older communities, and they have a completeness and a unity not found possible in museums of originals. Such collections must undoubtedly in the future be the main dependence of our American fine-art institutions. For although much of value still awaits the spade of the archaeologist, as has been proved by the recent finds at Cyprus, Pergamos, Olympia, Ephesus, Hissarlik, Mycenae, Assos, and other places, and although archaeological expeditions will undoubtedly be fitted out by Americans to the further enrichment of our museums, yet we cannot hope to stock them adequately with antiquities. Chances of acquiring valuable collections of originals are rare and will become rarer."[8]

Looking back, we can easily point out reasons for misapprehension of the course American museums would follow, and ways in which history belied expectations, or rather the lack of them. A part of the error came from an overemphasis on "antiquities" and paintings of the older periods as the main substance of a museum. Even Oriental and European decorative arts were not widely accepted as of great interest and value, and certainly it occurred to no one in the museum world that within fifty years the high-ranking American museums would be proudly devoting rooms, floors, wings, and separate houses to the exhibition of American arts and crafts. In the field of antiquities, itself, especially Egyptian antiquities, the objects from excavations that were to accrue to American museums were probably underestimated. But it is not strange that no one guessed the extent to which social, economic, and political shifts would release treasures thought to be permanently fixed in Europe. At first through gifts and bequests from collectors and later also by direct purchase, American museums began to fill with original objects once thought to be beyond their highest hopes.

Collections of Casts

Nevertheless, that museum people at the end of the century guessed wrong about the future of American museums does not mean that they were wrong about the need for collections of reproductions and the educational value of such collections. At the time, museums of casts were necessary and important, artistically and educationally. During the two decades when they were being so eagerly brought together, Greek and Latin were still studied; classical culture was still a lively part of education. In Norwich, for example, where a choice collection of reproductions was put to work under the classical genius of the Academy Principal and the experimental interest in art education of a young museum man, a long history of classical interest and "art-mindedness" resulted.

And even today, in the pride of our originals, we know that study collections of reproductions must be maintained for comparative purposes. Indeed the time may come, as one museum director has suggested, when the casts will be hauled up from the cellars and decently displayed in some central repository, some accessible American Trocadero.

NOTES

[1] The article, published in the *Nation* for November 21, 1889, also appeared in the New York *Evening Post* of November 23, 1889, and was reprinted in the *American Architect and Building News,* vol. 27, January 11, 1890, pp. 23-24. The articles were not signed, but in a pamphlet dated January, 1900 (see above, pp. 104-105), I mentioned an article "in the *Nation* for November, 1889, by Mr. Edward Robinson on 'The Cost of a Small Museum.'" The *Nation* files also attribute the article to "E. Robinson."

[2] Winifred E. Howe, *History of The Metropolitan Museum of Art,* [vol. I], New York: The Metropolitan Museum of Art, 1913, p. 252.

[3] Miss Beatrice Howe, Assistant Director of the Albright Art Gallery, very kindly helped me with the facts and figures given above.

[4] *Thirty-ninth Annual Report of the City Library Association, Springfield, Mass.... For the Year Ending May 1, 1900,* pp. 11-12, 32. I am indebted for help in bringing together this material to Mr. Hiller C. Wellman, Librarian of the City Library Association, and Mrs. John D. Pond, Director of the George Walter Vincent Smith Art Gallery.

[5] The present Director of the Department of Fine Arts, Mr. Homer Saint-Gaudens, and his staff have kindly answered questions as to dates and figures and helped with material from the Institute files.

[6] Miss Gertrude S. Hyde, Professor Emeritus of the Department of Art of Mount Holyoke College and a graduate of the Norwich Academy and Art School, kindly called these facts to my attention.

[7] *Library Journal,* vol. 17, November, 1892, pp. 457-458.

[8] *American Architect and Building News,* vol. 18, October 31, 1885, pp. 209-210.

THE GROLIER CLUB

In 1900 I reluctantly left Norwich and its Academy and went to The Grolier Club in New York, then at 29 East Thirty-second Street, where I was to be greatly interested in all I saw and experienced, and very happy also. The position was given me through the friendly influence of Bowen W. Pierson, who had been one of my friends in Norwich. I began work on September 1, as Assistant Librarian, the Librarian being Richard Hoe Lawrence, a member; early in 1903 I was appointed Librarian — a great honor for the boy from Boston's public library. The duties were different from those in a museum and not along the lines of a regular library. The object of the Club, its Constitution says, "shall be the literary study and promotion of the arts pertaining to the production of books, including the occasional publication of books designed to illustrate, promote and encourage those arts; and the acquisition, furnishing and maintenance of a suitable club building for the safe-keeping of its property, wherein meetings, lectures and exhibitions shall take place from time to time, likewise designed to illustrate, promote and encourage those arts and suitable for the purposes of the Club." The Library was the heart of the Club's activities and interests.

My friends wondered why I went to The Grolier Club. I suspect it was with the hope that I might go on to the Metropolitan Museum, which, ultimately, I did, but I learned much here that was of the greatest service to me afterwards, exhibition especially being one of the Club's functions as it is of the museum.

The Club was comprised largely of book collectors and bibliophiles, a word used by Thomas Frognall Dibdin and the French of his time and at first one in ill favor, though that attitude was short-lived, as it deserved to be. The members were distinguished men, some of them great bookmen, like Robert Hoe, William F. Havemeyer, Beverly Chew, William Loring Andrews, and Samuel P. Avery.

It was a different New York in those days, much more quiet and sedate. Nobody lived above Forty-second Street, the fashionable part being Murray Hill. The Waldorf-Astoria was at Thirty-fourth Street and Fifth Avenue. The Club-house in Thirty-second Street was within easy reach of its members, who came to it frequently in this period. The Club was presided over by Joseph L. Morton, who was a character, and Peter and his wife, who were good cooks.

The house itself was a dwelling-house, done over to suit the needs of the Club, with a large exhibition room built as an addition in the rear, but it had a good deal of style besides that which its collections and furniture gave it. The Library was housed in the top-floor rooms. 114 The other rooms were for the members' use.

Mr. Andrews, Mr. Avery, and Mr. Hoe were much interested in the furniture, made by a New York cabinetmaker — modern, I suppose we would call it, influenced by the William Morris movement, and I dare say that the furniture in the Club-house, which had so much individuality — certainly the Morris chairs and sofas — was ordered by them. The house in Thirty-second Street was also full of touches showing the influence of the bibliophiles of Paris and London — a charming place it was. When in 1917 the Club moved to its new building, 47 East Sixtieth Street, built by Bertram Goodhue, I superintended the transfer of the furniture and books of the Library, and I arranged them as nearly as possible in the way they were arranged in the old house. Those of us who had helped Goodhue with his plan for the new building — Harris Colt, Howard Mansfield, and I — saw to it that it copied, as far as possible, the old house and its floor plans. The Library, following my suggestion, copied in its scheme the best of the old college libraries of Oxford, with bookcases like those of Queen's College and lecterns like Merton's. E. G. Kennedy hung the framed engravings as they had been hung in the old house, in the halls, stairways, and rooms, and Mr. Avery's gift, the painting of "Grolier in the House of Aldus," I placed as it had been hung by him in the Thirty-second Street house, over the platform in the Lecture Room, where I hope it may always remain, as the so-to-say trademark of the Club.

The new house had more rooms in it than the old one, the Library, of course, was made much of, with busts of Theodore De Vinne, Edward G. Kennedy and others on the bookcases, and there was a room devoted to the storage of prints and the books on this subject — the collection now being large enough to warrant it. The delightful *Tapperij,* a copy of an old Dutch room, designed and given by Edwin Holden, was reinstalled, but its usefulness nowadays seems to have gone, the suppers cooked by the members after Council meetings having been given up, more's the pity. Habits established by the founders of clubs should never be allowed to fall into disuse. Such habits help to give them their character.

Brander Matthews, Professor at Columbia, wrote an account of The Grolier Club in 1889 which covers its character and purpose better than anything else. This article, published in the *Century Magazine*,[1] was afterwards reprinted, and if there are still people who make fun of those who study the book as an object in itself and pay attention to its physical appearance, they might well read it.

The enthusiastic study of printing and the other book arts, the writing about them, and the collecting of examples of them, revived in France and England in the nineteenth century at about the same time, and many distinguished names appear as practitioners. There had always been collectors of books, whose activities enriched the libraries of Europe; but now, through the efforts of these bibliophiles, the physical book became an important matter, and its history, printing, illustration, and binding began to receive great attention. A great bibliography soon took shape devoted to these subjects, and the movement had the desired influence and effect.

All of this history was the mainspring of the Club's activities, and the governing feature in the Club Library's accessions. In my day the Library possessed most of the books on typography listed in Bigmore and Wyman's *Bibliography of Printing*. Besides the bibliographical books and works on the book arts, the Club had a large collection of objects illustrative of printing, especially prints, bookbindings, sculpture, medals, and engravings. The Club's members have ever been most generous in their gifts of books and prints for the Library, Messrs. William Loring Andrews, Samuel P. Avery, and E. G. Kennedy especially so, and I believe it may be said that nowhere outside of Paris or London could the subjects of the Club be studied so well as in its Library. Its exhibitions, too, held from time to time, of material from its collections and loans from the members, furthered the study of bibliography and the interests of the Club.

In 1944, Miss Ruth Granniss and I were asked to address the Club, she on its exhibitions and I on its iconographic collections.[2] Reading Miss Granniss's address now, I am amazed at the number, quality, and impressiveness of the exhibitions, and I cannot but feel that in them alone a book-minded person could find education.

The publications of The Grolier Club, always influenced by France, were models of the art of printing, illustration, and binding. The Club's printing set the fashion for excellence in this country. Theodore L.

De Vinne, who was the most accomplished and learned of New York printers, did the Club's books for years and he was succeeded by Walter Gilliss, the Secretary of the Club, whose work was as perfect as De Vinne's but perhaps with more beauty. Bruce Rogers and D. B. Updike followed in due course.

Robert Hoe, the manufacturer of rotary printing presses and a great Francophile, was responsible for the establishment of the "Club Bindery," to which he and his bibliophile friends sent their books to be bound by the French binders they brought over from Paris to work for them. Mr. Hoe and Beverly Chew set the pace for that sort of work. The binders were the descendants of generations of workers in France. The Club members were also responsible for the revival of the use of engraved and printed bookplates, and for the employment of engravers in this delicate work, Edwin Davis French and Joseph Winfred Spenceley among them.

The Club has exerted a great influence in the study of bibliography and typography and has led to an improvement in the printing of the country through the study of its history, and the development of a critical taste in such matters in its membership. The things the Club stood for certainly influenced John Cotton Dana, then Librarian of the Newark Library, and me and led us to do a series of books which we called "The Literature of Libraries." There were six volumes in the set, printed by D. B. Updike in his best manner, with a title-page by T. M. Cleland. Each book contained a translation of a famous book or chapter on libraries,

with introductions by me or Miss Granniss. They were
printed on large paper, as well as small paper. Although they were not published until 1906 and 1907,
when I was at the Metropolitan, they were undertaken
in The Grolier Club days. An advance notice of the
series appeared in the *Library Journal* as early as
February, 1904.

Five more volumes, called "The Librarian's Series,"
were printed by Dana's brother at The Elm Tree Press
in Woodstock, Vermont, between 1909 and 1916.
Among these was a volume called *The Old Librarian's
Almanack,* written by Edmund L. Pearson, which was
really a literary forgery as it claimed to be a first re-
printing of a "very rare pamphlet first published in
New Haven, Connecticut in 1773," by one Philobib-
los, or Jared Bean. It got most favorable reviews in the
New York *Sun,* the *Nation,* the *Outlook,* the *Dial,* and
other journals, which to our amusement treated it as a
genuine old performance.

Dana had set up a printing press in his Library in
Newark, and he printed very amusing and interesting
things there. Among them was a broadside translating
an article on the "Librarian" from Etienne Gabriel
Peignot's *Dictionnaire raisonné de bibliologie.* He
also printed as a broadside a reflection which he entitled "This Our Noble Art" and said was "From
the Latin of Cardelius. 1546." This led to a series of
letters on the supposed author addressed to the *Nation*
by Robert Restieaux (H.W. K.), Harmon Karl (Edward H. Virgin), the Respectful Enquirer (Miss Ruth
Granniss), and Beverley Buncombe (Edmund L. Pear-

son), and an explanation of the real origin of the sentence by Dana. Afterwards, all the letters were printed in a little pamphlet by *The Printing Art*.

My years in The Grolier Club were happy and fruitful of many ideas which became a part of my stock in trade when I did eventually become a museum person. I learned there to know the importance of the book arts, and the beauty to be found in them — in printing, engraving, and binding. I learned also the value of good bibliographies and catalogues and how to use and make them, an accomplishment that was to stand me in good stead. My previous library experience led me to draw up what was essential to the cataloguing of the Club's books, a classification system for this bibliographical group, a matter not attempted in Dewey's decimal system. This tentative classification scheme was printed in the Club's year book in 1901, as a separate pamphlet in the same year, and finally in revised form in 1910, as *The Classification Used in the Library of The Grolier Club*. The *Library Journal* called it an "interesting detailed scheme of classification for bibliography, the book arts, and allied classes of literature." The main classes were: General Bibliography; Bibliography, The Book; Writing, Palaeography; Typography; Book Illustration, Engraving; Bookbinding; Ex Libris; Fine Arts; Literature; Biography, Portraits, Iconography, Miscellaneous.

One part of my job, besides the regular librarian performances, was helping with the Club's exhibitions and, occasionally, writing the catalogues which De Vinne printed for them. Among these were *Selected*

Works of the Poets Laureate of England (1901), and *One Hundred Books Famous in English Literature* (1902), for which Professor Woodberry of Columbia wrote the analysis of the authors, which was published in one volume, and I compiled bibliographical notes, which were published in 1903 as a second volume. For this catalogue, I went to England to consult books in the British Museum and the Bodleian Library at Oxford, and I came away with my pockets full of notes, Alfred Pollard helping me, that could not have been found elsewhere. The catalogues for the exhibitions of *Mosaic Bookbindings* (1902) and *Silver, Embroidered, and Curious Bookbindings* (1903) were the first books on these subjects. *Books, Engravings, Water-Colors, & Sketches by William Blake* (1905) was a catalogue of the third Blake exhibition in this country and the first to include many of his books, all lent by Club members, among them Robert Hoe, Marsden J. Perry, and William A. White of Brooklyn.

Many of the members of the Club, amateurs as well as professionals, became my friends, especially Mr. William Loring Andrews, who did so much for the student of New York prints, and Mr. Samuel P. Avery.

Mr. Andrews was a most discriminating amateur and collector, as well as author. Although an early collector of Chinese porcelain in New York, he is known rather for his books on matters connected with the history of New York, especially those that could be illustrated by prints, of which he was a prime collector. His enthusiasm infected many men and led to their collecting. It led also to the formation of the Society of Iconophiles, and the great enthusiasm of its members. I. N. Phelps Stokes's great publication on the iconography of New York owed its being to Mr. Andrews, and so did R. T. Haines Halsey's print collecting.

Mr. Andrews's study in his house in East Thirty-eighth Street was a delightful place, filled with illustrations of his interests, engravings of New York, and, I remember, a silver teapot by Paul Revere. It was such a room as would have been used by a French bibliophile.

Mr. Avery's study had this look, also, and Mr. Hoe's whole house, which was filled with his great library, was French in its feeling. All of the silver on the sideboard in his dining room was by Lamerie. I used to go to his house when an exhibition was under way, and in the morning would find him at breakfast, with Lamerie dishes in front of him and a French poodle on a chair on either side of him.

Mr. Avery started life as an engraver on wood, but gave that up to become a dealer in the arts. He was one of the first to sell the paintings of the artists of the Barbizon School to the millionaire collectors. His benefactions to Columbia College Library and the New York Public Library showed him to be ahead of his contemporaries in his understanding of the educational value of the arts and of books. His gift to the Public Library embraced prints by Whistler, Jacquemart, Bracquemond, Millet, and Seymour Haden, which, by his provision in his gift, were to be lent to the Club whenever wanted for its exhibitions.

122   Mr. Avery was the kindest of men, always thinking

of things to give one pleasure. I remember his taking me to a great dinner meeting of the Typothetae at Delmonico's, when Mr. De Vinne made the principal address, and Paul Leicester Ford, whom I knew from Norwich days, spoke on Franklin. Ford said that he had been asked if he had ever found anything in Franklin's writings to confirm the statements about his attitude towards women. He said no, he had not, except perhaps an entry in a diary, which read, "6 d. to the chambermaid."

Mr. Hoe, Mr. De Vinne, Mr. Andrews, and Mr. Avery were all presidents of the Club at one time or another, and all helped to give it the characteristics we associate with it. A French bibliophile coming to New York would have felt quite at home in the Club-house, reflecting as it did so many things the French had originated.

I must not forget to mention two other members and presidents. One was Edward G. Kennedy, dealer in prints and the best of storytellers, also a friend of Whistler. I helped to make his great and complete catalogue of Whistler's etchings, but if I failed to mention the least scratch in a trial proof, I was reprimanded. The other was Beverly Chew, the great collector of Elizabethan literature; his constant kindness is to be remembered, and his knowledge of the texts of his books as well as their bibliographical details. It was he who inaugurated the series called "Collations and Notes"[3] and who initiated the Club's series of exhibitions embracing the bibliography of certain authors.

One of the most distinguished members of the Club,

whom I remember with great pleasure and who ought never to be forgotten, was General Rush C. Hawkins, the organizer of the Hawkins' Zouaves in the Civil War. He was a collector of the first issues of the first presses in Europe after the invention of printing, and made a most notable collection, which he gave to the library he founded in memory of his wife, The Annmary Brown Memorial in Providence. His acquaintance with the great French collectors of incunabula was remarkable. I spent a never-to-be-forgotten holiday with him once in Paris.

Another interesting frequenter of the Club was Joseph Pennell, the illustrator. I remember him vividly because of his rivalry with Edward G. Kennedy, my friend Richard Canfield, and Freer of Detroit as the chief friend of Whistler, whose biography Pennell and his wife wrote. I have no doubt but that that honor was held by Canfield, though Kennedy could put forward strong claims for the distinction. Canfield was not a member of the Club, but he was a book collector of an unusual kind. He undertook to acquire all the great monuments of English literature in perfect condition, but finding this to be impossible, he gave it up. His friend, Marsden Perry of Providence, was a member and brought together one of the finest of Shakespeare libraries. His loans to the Club's Blake exhibition helped to make it unique.

The acquaintance with such men as these Club members, as well as other collectors, illustrators, bookbinders, publishers, and booksellers who visited and used the Library, some of the greatest, here and abroad, was an education in itself. My acquaintance with printers, T. L. De Vinne, Berkeley Updike of Boston, Walter Gilliss, Bruce Rogers, Frederic Warde, Carl P. Rollins among them, the best we have produced, all young then, except De Vinne, but all well known now, also began at this time, and gave me great pleasure.

Of The Grolier Club members and presidents none was so remarkable as that great printer, student of printing, and writer on typography, Theodore L. De Vinne. He was the first to advance typography from the place it occupied in the country as a mere craft to a place of importance as an art. He was unaffected by the excitement which William Morris aroused in printers everywhere, because he knew more about typography than Morris did and had greater respect for it. All of his own many books were contributions to the subject. He printed the *Century Magazine* in its heyday, and indeed it is not too much to say that his work influenced the printers and publishers of the whole country.

I remember one lesson Mr. De Vinne gave me. He had written a book on the Italian printers of the Renaissance, which The Grolier Club published. It was his last book, and he was anxious to have it perfect, so he offered a prize to his proofreaders, if a mistake should be found at the last minute. He asked Miss Granniss and me also to read the proofs, and, of course, he read them himself. When the book was finished and ready to be distributed, he, not any of us, found a misprint! He said that the old saying that no book was ever free of errors was quite right.

Walter Gilliss, Secretary of the Club, was also distinguished, for the technical perfection of his work and for its elegance. He designed and printed Mr. Andrews's charming books; and his printing of Stokes's *Iconography of New York* was a *tour de force,* remarkable in its handling of all the complicated typographical problems. He, too, felt it unnecessary to let his work be changed by the influence William Morris was exerting on others at this time. Afterwards, Gilliss helped me with the Museum publications, setting their standards of excellence.

Later, as a member of the Club and on its Committee on Publications, I was able to suggest the names of two other printers, friends of mine, Bruce Rogers and D. B. Updike, as men who could give the Club publications variety and greater interest. I was happy to be able to suggest the name of Rudolph Ruzicka also as the engraver for a book on New York, with text by Walter Prichard Eaton; it became one of the most noteworthy books ever printed on the subject. John Dana was quick to see the advantages of a similar book of scenes in Newark and to ask Ruzicka to make the engravings for it.

I was fortunate in having as my assistant in the Club Ruth Shepard Granniss, a graduate of the Pratt Institute Library School, who succeeded me as Librarian. She dropped into the Club position as if it had been made for her, being well fitted for it by training and interest. Her work for the Club, especially her writing for the catalogues and her public addresses, did a great deal to make the Club's vocation clear to the unbibliographically minded.

Two friends of The Grolier Club days, who were active in Club matters, afterwards became active in Metropolitan Museum affairs. R. T. Haines Halsey, a collector of Americana, who devoted himself especially to silversmiths and their work, during the building of the American Wing, having now become a Trustee of the Museum, assumed the task of the installation of the rooms and their furnishings. William M. Ivins, Jr., who in the Club was helpful in the exhibitions of prints, he being an expert in their history, trained in Germany, became the first Curator of the Museum's Department of Prints, and created a remarkable collection.

While working in the Club, I came to know Dr. John Shaw Billings, the first Librarian of the Public Library in its last days in the Astor Library building and its first days in the new building on Fifth Avenue, and through him the distinguished men of that world of books, Lydenberg, Eames, Paltsits, and Weitenkampf. Dr. Billings had been a visitor in Norwich when I was there, a friend of David A. Wells. He had no use for bibliophiles, and, like so many of their detractors, did not hesitate to say so, but, to my surprise, he asked me to talk to the Public Library's staff and trustees on bookbinding! To illustrate my speech and to the distress of the librarian in charge, Wilberforce Eames, I was allowed to pull many rare books in fine covers off the shelves of the Lenox Library, where they were jammed in helter-skelter. These books, its treasures, are now kept in a showcase of the building at Forty-second Street. Afterwards I wrote a catalogue for the

Library of its great collection of books "in fine bindings," in the Spencer Collection.

As I noted when writing about the Library School,
Mr. Dewey was not interested in bibliophilism or in
any of the things The Grolier Club stood for, and the
lack of training in such subjects has ever been obvious
in library people. For this reason I was glad to associate
myself with the New York Library Club. First they
made me Treasurer, for which I was in no way fitted,
and then President, in 1905. During my term in that
office, such subjects as printing, book illustration,
bookbinding, and bibliography were played up by
various speakers, including Ingalls Kimball and Henry
Lewis Johnson. Agnes Repplier spoke at one meeting.

During the period when I was at The Grolier Club,
I was elected a member of the Century Club, proposed by Edmund Clarence Stedman and seconded by
General Edward Harland of Norwich, the Norwich
clockmaker's grandson, old friends whose graciousness
was greatly appreciated.

The Century Club in those days proved to be interesting. There was still a remainder of the traditional
literary and artistic group for which it was famous. I
was counted as a librarian, but later I was looked upon,
because of my Metropolitan Museum association, as
belonging to the class now called the curator or museum group. Mr. Stedman asked me to luncheon with
him after my election, and he showed me the various
rooms and the library. We looked into the small room
devoted to the Graham Library, and he said, "Some
day, when you get to be famous, you may come in here

and drink your after-dinner coffee." It is needless to say that I have never enjoyed that privilege. Dr. Austin Flint, Beverly Chew, Charles R. Miller, Editor of the New York *Times,* and their friends sat at the head of the long dining-room table, and with their basso-profundo voices dominated the talk in the room. John La Farge sat by himself at a side table with his bottle of iced champagne beside him, and no one spoke to him unless asked to do so.

Cocktails were then becoming a habit before dinner, but those who took two were carefully remarked. Salads were generally eaten, each man dressing his own, but at this performance no one could equal Hopkinson Smith, whose ability to make various combinations of greens and a remarkable variety of dressings required a grand array of pots and kettles around his plate and the attention of everyone at table. Wine and even whisky and soda were seldom drunk at table except by La Farge, and it was not until Ingalls Kimball undertook to create the habit that the fashion changed. The Club's library, for which Dr. John Billings drew up a classification, was difficult to use, and its librarian in my early days was a bartender who had been promoted. Shades of Melvil Dewey! I used to spend my time there reading Pierre Bayle's Dictionary, until an active committee threw out his folio volume for more and less interesting books.

A delightful friend of those days was Auguste Jaccaci, a mixture of Hungarian and Italian, an illustrator, and a devoted disciple of the book arts. He seemed to know everybody, here and abroad, and was most generous in sharing his friendships. When Rogers and I were printing our little book, *Amycus et Célestin,* in his new Centaur types, it was Jaccaci who got the permission of Anatole France to do it, and it was he who helped me persuade the modest Bryson Burroughs, who did the illustrations for the book which Timothy Cole cut on wood in the Italian manner, to hold the first exhibition of his work. Burroughs was trained in the studio of Puvis de Chavannes in Paris, as a mural painter, but the demand for such work not being great, he took to doing easel pictures in his own inimitable manner. When Roger Fry came to the Metropolitan Museum as Curator of Paintings, I recommended Burroughs as his Assistant. This position Burroughs filled helpfully, and he ultimately succeeded Fry as Curator, carrying on that work with real distinction.

Jaccaci and I used to breakfast together every Sunday morning at the Café Lafayette, when he would bring something he had written to read aloud to those who were our guests there. I remember it was he who really introduced me to Chinese art, taking me to Loo's place, then on Fifth Avenue opposite the Library, to see some marvelous bronzes. No memories are happier than those connected with Jaccaci.

I was also for a time a member of The Players, where I met a new kind of friends, and most entertaining ones, among them James L. Ford, the senior newspaper critic of plays, Richard Mansfield, the actor, and many other literary people and actors. The Players Club was delightful, and I regretted having to resign. Clubs usu-

ally teach little or nothing except a certain form of

social behavior, but The Players introduced me to such real matters as plays and players, and the arts of writing and acting.

I enjoyed myself thoroughly at The Grolier Club; the work was just up my alley, and I hated to leave. Happily, my association with the Club continued after I went to the Metropolitan Museum. In 1906 I was elected a resident member of the Club and in 1930 an honorary member. I served on the Council of the Club from 1908 to 1928, as its President from 1920 to 1924, and at different times as member of the Committee on Publications, the Library Committee, the Committee on Arrangements, and various special committees.

In 1909 and 1910, the members of the Club gave two plays, performed by the members themselves, both wisely chosen to add interest to the subjects of the Club. One was *Depositio Cornuti Typographici,* an old German Morality, often played at the initiation of apprentices into the printing trade; the other was Thackeray's little satire called *Reading a Poem.* Both were admirably done, and I had a part in each. Updike printed the plays in his best manner.

The Grolier Club taught me what I think I had never known before, what I find few people seem to know, the importance of bibliography to the educated, or shall we say cultivated, person. One reads books, but few read the bibliography of the subjects the books treat of. A history of the invention of printing is interesting and of great value, but a bibliography of the books on that subject is of greater value.

Largely owing to the influence of The Grolier

131

Club, the American Institute of Graphic Arts was founded in 1914, to stimulate and encourage those engaged in the graphic arts. This organization has been of real value in the community, and has got nearer to the *worker* in the book arts than The Grolier Club has done. I had the pleasure of being the President of the Institute for three years, 1936 to 1938. A gold medal is given annually to men who have distinguished themselves by their services, and I was so fortunate as to receive one in 1930. The citation, written by Frederic G. Melcher, suggests some of the aims of the Institute, and some of the results of my own education. I blush to quote his kind words:

CITATION ON THE PRESENTATION TO
HENRY WATSON KENT OF THE MEDAL OF THE
AMERICAN INSTITUTE OF GRAPHIC ARTS
FEBRUARY 4, 1930

The American Institute of Graphic Arts has achieved its purposes through a significant decade by developing the public taste, by giving designers the stimulation of competition, and by finding ways to honor those who have signally served.

For its first purpose it has used traveling exhibits, for the second provided competent juries, for the third established an Institute Medal to be awarded to those whom it desires to honor, for on their genius depends the progress of American art. This Medal is bestowed on the suggestion of a special Committee of Award and by the vote of the Board of Directors. It is not connected with an exhibit of a special achievement except as the exhibit may be the occasion to bring the members together. It expresses our appreciation of a career of notable influence in the field of graphic arts. No bestowal could be more in harmony with the spirit of the Medal than its award to-night to Henry Watson Kent, friend of artists, wise counsellor in the Institute's development, secretary of the Metropolitan Museum of Art, director of the Museum's press.

Mr. Kent has been a touchstone of good taste to a generation of artists, he knows and understands the best of the old and has inspired the best of the new. He added a touch to the printing of an art museum, and it became itself an accompanying art; books of the Press have been models for many. He has stood for a broad interpretation of a museum's functions, and its exhibits have reached designers and craftsmen in the midst of trade fairs, its bulletins and handbooks have increased the circle of art's influence.

Though his interests have included all arts (he has even collected meeting houses) he has had the deepest influence on typography. He was a friend and admirer of De Vinne, helping to spread the popular understanding of that great master's ideals for the craft; he worked closely with Gilliss on his impeccable publications for the Museum and for The Grolier Club. He was prompt with appreciation for the printing of Updike and Rogers, he gave encouragement and opportunity to Cleland and to Rollins, he has been a guide and inspiration to Silvé, to Wood, to Fass and others. His gifts of understanding have made him a critic who can still remain a friend. He has given sound counsel, discerning appreciation and treasures of rarest friendship.

In England, such a one has recently been publicly honored by the bestowal of knighthood on Emery Walker; in our country equal appreciation is the due of Henry Watson Kent, who, as reads the inscription on this Gold Medal of the Institute "has had a lifelong influence on the graphic arts."

NOTES

The Grolier
Club

[1] *Century Magazine*, vol. 39, November, 1889, pp. 87-97. Reprinted in Brander Matthews, *Bookbindings Old and New: Notes of a Book-Lover, with an Account of The Grolier Club of New York*. New York: Macmillan and Co., 1895.

[2] R. S. Granniss, *The Grolier Club and Its Exhibitions*, New York: The Grolier Club, 1944; H. W. Kent, *The Grolier Club and Its Iconographic Collections*, New York: The Grolier Club, 1944.

[3] The first volume of this series was issued in 1893 with the title: *Catalogue of Original and Early Editions of some of the Poetical and Prose Works of English Writers from Langland to Wither: With Collations & Notes*. . . . Three further volumes were issued in 1905, being a similar catalogue of the works of English writers from Wither to Prior.

THE METROPOLITAN
MUSEUM OF ART

I REMAINED IN The Grolier Club until 1905, when I was given the position of Assistant Secretary to help Robert W. de Forest, then Secretary of The Metropolitan Museum of Art and after 1913 its President. Professor Ware was quite right, the Museum had arrived at the point where it did need young men. General Cesnola's staff was made up of men of middle age, without training in museum work. When he died, in November, 1904, he left behind him three curators. There was no love lost among these gentlemen. I remember that, one day, one of them invited another to "come outside," which he did, but to argue, not to fight. The one chased the other all around through the galleries. I called the policeman at the door, and he stopped the exciting performance. I have never known professional feelings to run so high. The General's secretary, who was asked to turn over the records to me, regarded me as an interloper; he dumped all the Museum records and letters, which were docketed in the old-fashioned way and bound up with red tape, in a vault helter- 135 skelter. My first job was to sort these papers, flatten them out, and catalogue and file them in new-fashioned filing cases of Dewey's devising. The Registrar was an Irishman, who carried a Latin Bible in his pocket, from which he would ask you to read passages, to test your scholarship.

A room about as big as a closet was given me for my office, and here my secretary, H. F. Davidson, and I sat and roasted in summer. We seldom took a vacation and we began work, unlike the lordly curators, at a quarter before nine each day. Most of the rooms in that old building, Wing B, as it was called, were originally intended for exhibition galleries (no suite of offices was thought of by the architect). As galleries they had no outside air or light until, a few years after my going to the Museum, windows were cut in the walls through solid stone to convert them into needed offices.

There was only one telephone in the place, in the Library, to which we had to run when we were called, and a typewriter was come by with difficulty. There was a restaurant in the building, presided over by an Italian of Cesnola's choosing, and the food was quite celebrated, the *fritto misto* and spaghetti especially. There was a "Director's Dining Room," where Cesnola used to eat, with any Trustee who happened to be present.

The year 1905 marked the beginning of a new era in the Museum's history. The years of early efforts, with all that was done to make clear its meaning and the place it should occupy in the city, may be said to have ended with the death of General Cesnola. In those

ANNO DOMINI MCMXXVI

THE MUSEUM PRESS
BIDS YOU WELCOME
TODAY AND
EVERY
DAY

Mr. Kent as printer and host

AT A MEETING OF
THE BOARD OF TRUSTEES
OF
THE METROPOLITAN MUSEUM OF ART
HELD OCTOBER 18, 1926
THE GIFT OF
THE LORD CARNARVON COLLECTION
OF EGYPTIAN ART
FROM
EDWARD STEPHEN HARKNESS
WAS ACCEPTED WITH GRATEFUL THANKS
AND WITH AN EXPRESSION
OF APPRECIATION
OF ITS VALUE TO THE MUSEUM
AND ITS PLACE IN
THE HISTORY OF ART

Folder on handmade paper, 9 x 12½ inches, designed by
Mr. Kent and printed at The Museum Press.

years the Museum's legal status and its civic place were worked out and its aims emphasized, especially those in the Charter in the phrase which reads, "of encouraging and developing the study of the fine arts." It had obtained some recognition of what it intended to do, had accumulated some works of art, and had given the people some idea of the importance of art as a civic benefit. It must be remembered that art in those early days was looked at a little askance and had to prove its usefulness. As to any practical value in it, except for artists and students of the history of art, though the theory had been advanced, for instance by Joseph H. Choate in 1880 at the opening of the Museum building in Central Park, it had not yet been acted upon. In spite of all difficulties, however, the Museum's Board of Trustees as well as its Director had worked hard to bring their plans to reality, and the new regime had the benefit of a good foundation to build on.

The setup of 1905 was strikingly new in personnel and strong in character. Toward the close of 1904, J. Pierpont Morgan became President of the Museum, Robert W. de Forest Secretary, and John Crosby Brown Treasurer. Soon after my arrival in the Museum, Sir Caspar Purdon Clarke was appointed Director and Edward Robinson Assistant Director. Sir Caspar Purdon Clarke had been the Art Director of the South Kensington Museum, an architect, and a student of the art and architecture of India, where he had lived and worked with Rudyard Kipling's father in teaching Indians South Kensington manners and customs. Sir Purdon was a delightful person, full of friendliness and

137

good nature, winning friends for the Museum right and left. His experience in the South Kensington Museum with its organization and its manners so different from ours caused him to rely upon others to a large degree (my secretary, Davidson, was given to him for his help), but if he did nothing else during his too short term of office, he made the Museum seem a friendly place. Edward Robinson, who came from Boston to assist Sir Purdon, brought to his position the advantages he had gained as a classical scholar and the first trained museum man. He gave to the Museum, when he assumed the directorship in 1910, the dignity of the scholar with wide knowledge and associations and a keen sense of the Museum's purpose.

Money, too, was beginning to come to the Museum in greater amounts, by bequest and gift. The opportunity was at hand to do all sorts of things which had not been done before, an opportunity not to be neglected.

In going to the Metropolitan Museum, I was conscious that a good knowledge of the arts it collected and their histories was an advantage, but I realized that while this kind of knowledge was necessary for curators, it was not required for an assistant secretary, and accordingly I applied my mind to the problem of just what was his field besides keeping minutes and sending out notices of meetings, the doing of which could not occupy all his time. So I studied the Constitution, and in it I saw ways of being useful, even if not a curator or an authority on artistic subjects. What I had learned in the Columbia Library School, in the

138

Norwich museum, in The Grolier Club, and in my study of European museums could be put to work here, and Mr. de Forest was complaisant and willing to let me try out new ideas.

At this time, I was living in Washington Square, in the house on the east side, number 80, called The Benedick. It was famous as the first bachelors' apartment house in New York, built by McKim, Mead & White, and famous also as the setting for the opening scene of Edith Wharton's *House of Mirth*. This building was diagonally opposite Mr. de Forest's house, number 7, on the north side of the Square, and a more perfect arrangement for a secretary and his assistant could not have been contrived. I stopped in at number 7 frequently mornings on my way to the Museum, while Mr. de Forest was at breakfast, when we had discussions on every problem and proposition that came up. Such visits were also made at Mr. de Forest's office in the Johnston Building in Broad Street, and, when he was in the country, at his house in Cold Spring Harbor. I believe these frequent meetings were responsible for our close attention to all problems and their solutions.

I have been attempting to tell about the things and people that gave me my education, my knowledge of museums — what was needed for them, what to do and how to do it; but when I became associated with Mr. de Forest, I learned more of skill and wisdom in the handling of such affairs than I had ever thought of before. His willingness to listen to his assistant and his answers to questions were models of patience. His quick "Yes" or "No" or "Go ahead" or "See what you can do" were as heartening as they were brief. In 1913, when Mr. de Forest was made President, I was elected Secretary, nominated by Mr. George F. Baker. This position I could never have filled except that Mr. de Forest, with all his kindness and wisdom, stood behind me. I owed everything to him.

The year 1948, as the centennial of Robert W. de Forest's birth, is an important anniversary in the history of museums. Mr. de Forest has often appropriately been referred to as New York's first citizen, because of his many and far-reaching contributions to the social and artistic welfare of the city. Through his membership on the Tenement House Commission, through his activity and far-sighted wisdom in the organization and administration of such institutions as the Charity Organization Society, the New York School of Social Work, the Welfare Council of New York, and the Russell Sage Foundation, his concern for the people of New York was expressed. His service to the Metropolitan Museum was governed not so much by the desire to show the best art that the Museum could buy as to give the citizens of New York the benefits which might come to them through the knowledge of art and how to enjoy it. What he did in the Metropolitan Museum, firmly based on this principle, influenced the other museums of the country. Among the many contributions which caused him to be so rightly called New York's first citizen, his thoughtful, understanding service to the people of New York and of the country through the Museum should never be forgotten.

As Assistant Secretary and Secretary, I sat in at all meetings of the Board of Trustees and took notes for the minutes I was to write. Mr. Morgan and later Mr. de Forest as President made admirable chairmen, and I believe no group of men could have been more thoughtful and understanding than this one, full of wisdom regarding the principles that should govern the actions of a Board entrusted with the management of a public institution.

The museum man, if he keeps his ears open, may learn much from his Trustees. I can never forget what lessons were set for me of wisdom and thoughtfulness by the distinguished men who formed our Board, especially by those who had that rarest of qualities to be found in men who have made their mark — a willingness to talk with the young man about matters of concern to all, of whatever degree or position. I must record my indebtedness to certain ones: Mr. John L. Cadwalader, Mr. Joseph H. Choate, Mr. Elihu Root, and Mr. Lewis Cass Ledyard, as well as Mr. de Forest. They all had this gift of generously imparting their wisdom to the youngster, in meetings and out.

One of the needs apparent to me from the very first was organization of the Museum's own executive work. General Cesnola was a dictator and kept everything in his own hands; for him no system was needed. The drawing up of a system to make the Museum's business run smoothly and effectively was a natural thing to do, the kind of thing any business house would do as an economic measure, if for no other reason. The making of a kind of machine which should allow the Museum 141 to carry on its work easily and intelligently, which should automatically inform all of the many employees what was being done and what they should know of such things, at the least expense and labor — this was a task that fell to me as the *entrepreneur* between the initiators of all action, the Trustees, and their employees. An account of the methods developed, which worked a great change in the administration of the Museum, was given at a meeting of the American Association of Museums in 1911, and was printed in its *Proceedings* and in the Museum *Bulletin* of that year. In 1926 it was reprinted as a pamphlet.

Central to this development of a system adapted to the rapid growth of the Museum was the card catalogue. Previously museums kept their records of accessions in big, ungainly books, but we determined to make a real catalogue, and to this end to adapt the card catalogue system, with which my library training had made me familiar, to the Museum's records, with a photograph of the object on the verso of the card and a description on the recto. Fortunately just about this time there began to be available sensitized cardboard that was guaranteed to last.

Several copies of these cards were made, for the accessions clerk, the curatorial department concerned, the Sales and Information Desk, and the general catalogue. The organization of the Catalogue Division, with the selection of the young college graduates who were to do the work under Miss Margaret A. Gash, a graduate of the Library School of Pratt Institute, was an important part of the system. Rules for cataloguing objects of art were worked out, a glossary of terms used in the various arts was compiled, and methods of co-operation between the curatorial departments and the Catalogue Division were developed. Thus some uniformity and consistency in cataloguing became possible, and the record of the Museum's possessions could be easily used by the public as well as by Museum people.

This system of cataloguing obviously necessitated the development of a Photographic Studio, and with the photographing for record of every new object except prints and reproductions, the making of photographic prints, enlargements, and lantern slides for sale and for Museum use rapidly became matter-of-course. Photographs of the temporary as well as the permanent exhibitions helped tell the story of changing methods and styles. In the special problems involved in photographing works of art, our photographer, Edward Milla, and his assistants became most skillful, and, with ever increasing equipment, the department was a model of its kind.

It was plain to see that a public institution of art was, in the last analysis, a public servant, and that the things to do were the things which worked for the public welfare. The old idea of the museum as a storehouse of art laid it open to the criticism that it would become a mausoleum in fact unless it was made to be actively serviceable. In other words, the European idea of a museum of art which housed the treasures the country had accumulated by hook or by crook, museums like the Vatican and the Louvre, did not fit the needs of this country, which had its own arts to develop. The American museum should show collections of what other civilizations had done, under religious or civil influences, of course, as a lesson to those whose business it was to produce similar kinds of things for us, to show what had been done and what might be done, by our own artists and craftsmen. Thus the museum would become a teacher in the truest sense, which was a new idea in this country — the active teacher instead of the inactive opportunity.

One could not sit in a museum of art and watch the people who visit it come and go without wondering why they came and what they expected to get from their visits. Early in my employment in the Metropolitan Museum I began to classify the groups according to what I found they wanted, or appeared to want. The classification looked like this.

1. The idle and curious, who came on holidays with their friends to see what it was all about.
2. The people who came with the desire to learn.
3. The real students of art and archaeology, who knew what they wanted and how to study.
4. The teachers and pupils of the public schools, who came because the School Board told them to do so.
5. The practical people, manufacturers and designers, who employed the arts of design as part of their business.
6. The artist who wanted to widen his knowledge, and the copyist.

7. Museum Members, who paid for their privileges or who inherited them.

Keeping in mind the needs of these various classes of visitors, we could see that certain kinds of help were necessary for each, and that certain other kinds of help were needed for all of them. We therefore set ourselves to providing what we thought was needed.

The Charter of the Museum had stated as its purpose that "of encouraging and developing the study of the fine arts, and the application of arts to manufactures and practical life, of advancing the general knowledge of kindred subjects, and, to that end, of furnishing popular instruction," but not all of these aims had yet been put into effect. The problem was, as I saw it, to devise ways of giving this popular education, which obviously must be by lectures, talks, and publications of a not too scholarly character, and by encouragement of people to use the collections under guidance until they learned to use them by themselves. (Artists, painters, and sculptors were supposed to know what they wanted and needed in the Museum and to be able to help themselves.) These things seemed to me to be the first things to be aimed at, and finding help and encouragement from Mr. de Forest and, later, from the Trustees' Committee on Educational Work, which came into being in 1912, I may say we were able to tackle the problem and to show results.

One of the pleasantest episodes in our early days of seeking to make the Museum useful to school teachers and pupils occurred in 1908, the year that the Museum appointed its first instructor. Having had a notice of

145

the Third International Art Congress for the Development of Drawing and Art Teaching, to be held in London, I asked its secretary if I might have the time and place in which to hold a session on museums and schools, the use of the institutions by school people. I was told that I might have Herbert Spencer's lecture room, but that I must provide my own chairman. Mr. de Forest was to be in Scotland motoring at the time, and he promised to come down and preside. Several people from the States attended the session, including Dr. James P. Haney, Director of Art in the New York High Schools, and two or three people then or later part of the Metropolitan Museum's educational staff. Roger Fry of London, Alfred Lichtwark of Hamburg, and a Russian who was interested in our subject spoke, and Mrs. Bernhard Berenson, who came in the place of her husband. The speakers were excellent, and we got much attention for them in the newspapers. The meeting was a real success. A gentleman who showed great interest in the program proved to be Viscount Sudeley, a member of the House of Lords. His interest resulted in an Act of Parliament and the appointment of "Guide Lecturers" for London museums, who were responsible for guidance of those who desired it and for help to teachers and school children; a society called by his name continued this work. Thus our efforts in New York had a wider influence.

The work with the New York schools promised to be of a rather uphill kind, teachers and pupils being busy with their own curricula and our kind of art not being thought of real importance; indeed few of the

The Metropolitan Museum of Art

146

teachers themselves at that time knew much about the history of art. But with the interest of Dr. Haney, Director of Art in the High Schools, and the help of the School Art League, which he founded and which went forward for many years under the guidance of Miss Florence N. Levy, results began to be seen, especially in the work with the Washington Irving High School. Several other people, too, showed understanding of what we were trying to do, but I learned that really effective co-operation could be gained only through the interest of the Board of Education itself and the usual machinery adopted by it for the introduction of a new subject. Until this should happen, the Trustees authorized the appointment of some really able person to act as what the schools called a Supervisor, to work between the Museum and the schools in the understood way, which would have made the relation official; but for one reason and another, the scheme was not carried out.

The Trustees in Cesnola's time had planned to meet the Charter's demand for popular education. They had organized an industrial school and an art school, and when the Central Park building was first occupied, they had set apart a gallery for the exhibition of industrial arts. Public lectures, also, had been given, one by our old friend Charles Eliot Norton. The schools had been given up long before I came to the Museum, for one reason or another, and the lectures were spasmodic, not an annual program, so that when I got there, there remained little of these efforts to carry on. Schools seemed to be out of the question — there were enough 147 of them in the town — but lectures might well be planned as a part of our new program. Few were given elsewhere, for art schools, it seemed, were not interested in the history of the arts.

After a time, formal lectures on art were arranged for Saturdays in the big classroom and Sundays in the new Lecture Hall — the former scholarly and the latter popular — and this service to the public grew into a thoughtful and carefully arranged one. Curiously enough, when we began to look for good lecturers on art, men like Kenyon Cox and Professor Mather, we found them few and far between. Those available were mostly college professors, who were not trained in public speaking, being used to talking to their students in classrooms in a conversational tone. But we taught them the need of clear, audible speech and effective presentation.

Lectures had long been one of the most popular forms of educating the public, the Lowell lectures in Boston being the model all copied. But such lectures as were there given needed no illustration — they were begun in 1839 before the stereopticon was in use. Lectures on art, it soon appeared, needed illustrations —they were as important as the text itself. We were fortunate in our period, when mechanical methods of reflecting pictures on a screen were being rapidly perfected, and in having a Photograph Department that could make lantern slides. In the first lectures in the Museum we used a reflectoscope, a machine into which books and prints could be laid and the illustrations reflected on a screen. The rapid development of the stereopticon, color slides, and motion pictures opened new possibilities in this work. It seemed a long time from the Norwich days, when the stereopticon was possible for only a few special lectures, to this period when projection techniques were constantly improving and becoming more generally usable.

For the students of art, who knew what they wanted and how to get it, there was, from the beginning, the Library, an excellent one, and, under the direction of William Clifford, a most helpful one. We established a reference collection of photographs, which came to contain everything of an illustrative kind relating to art, a lending collection of lantern slides, which was as rich in material as any in the country, and study rooms for the use of a student who desired to see objects not on exhibition and to study them. The student of art was well taken care of. Arrangements were also made with the help of New York University and the able head of its art department, Fiske Kimball, to give the professors and students in the city's colleges special privileges for lectures and study. Every facility was given copyists, including a room for their use.

While various sorts of lectures and talks were being experimented with and developed, education was also being carried on through publications small and large — handbooks, guides, and scholarly publications — and here too new ground was broken and new standards set. For our publications, also, we were lucky in the fact that illustrations now became comparatively cheap and easy to get because of the invention of mechanical processes for reproduction, especially the halftone. It be-

149

came clear that the more illustrations you gave your public the better it liked your lectures and publications, and the more useful they became.

In one sense, the Museum Press and the Editorial Division were a part of the educational work; in another, they belonged with the effort to improve the machinery, the business system, of the Museum's own organization. In General Cesnola's day all notices to Members and their bills were written by hand, well written by a man who did nothing else, all day long. The saving of time and money if such notices were printed was obvious. The man interested me, and I asked him if he knew how to set type. Though he said he did not, I put him to work at it, and he proved to be able to do anything with his hands — printing turned out to be easy for him. He stayed with us for the rest of his life, and helped to make the Press famous. James Doyle was his name, God rest his soul! We eventually got a full complement of machinery and did everything needed for the Museum except the *Bulletin* and books — posters, forms and blanks, invitations, pamphlets, and of course labels.

Good labels in a museum are essential, and therefore are one of such an institution's real problems, their unobtrusiveness, clearness, harmoniousness, and correct typography being a part of what must be looked out for. Before the typewriter came into use, the labels were handwritten, or printed in a job printing establishment. In either case they were poor. What information should be given on the label was a question that

was debated seriously by the American Association of

Museums, and of course the science people arrived at a decision long before the art museum folks did. This problem interested me, and I drew up rules for the placing of the facts to be given, following the rules the librarian used for his cards, but the Curators regarded the desire for uniformity in label arrangement as unimportant, and so this innovation took time. For one of the meetings of the Museums Association, Doyle and I made an exhibition of what could be done in printing labels — the use of various types, various papers and materials, and various colors of ink, and we printed a little guide to go with it, giving rules for the text and its arrangement.

My experience in The Grolier Club had taught me what I needed to know about types and styles in printing; and with Doyle's help we became quite famous. John Dana wrote us up, at length, and Bruce Rogers said complimentary things about our work. In his *Paragraphs on Printing* he spoke of the Museum Press as "a private press operating in a public capacity. Its output has always been of the highest distinction, whether posters for the Museum, exhibition cards, notices of meetings, testimonials, or other varieties of printing. They all bear the evidence of Mr. Kent's impeccable taste and profound knowledge of typography."[1] I think in typographical matters we had an influence on other museums.

In 1938 there came the highest and most unexpected tribute to the Museum printing, one that gave it real status. In the prefatory note to a volume of addresses made at the opening of an exhibition of work arranged in the Morgan Library, Miss Belle da Costa Greene, its Librarian and the sponsor of the honor, says: "In appreciation of the work initiated and furthered by Mr. Kent, in raising the standard of institutional printing to that of one of the Fine Arts, the Trustees of The Pierpont Morgan Library arranged that an Exhibition of Printing done by and for The Metropolitan Museum of Art, under the Supervision of Henry Watson Kent, should be held in that Library from October 26 to November 12, 1938. The following addresses were delivered on the evening of October 24 at the private view, held for the members of The American Institute of Graphic Arts." The material for the exhibition was selected by Lauder Greenway and William M. Ivins, Jr., and was arranged in the Library's great room of exhibitions by Rudolph Ruzicka and Miss Greene. The addresses at the private view were given by my friends D. B. Updike, Bruce Rogers, Carl P. Rollins, and William Ivins, and the volume was printed by Carl Rollins with special attractiveness as an American Institute of Graphic Arts Keepsake. Later the exhibition was sent to several other cities by the Institute. This high compliment gave me the greatest pleasure.

As two of the speakers at the exhibition of the Museum's printing observed, the work of the Editorial Division had much to do with the quality of the finished product. This department was built up with the greatest care under Miss Winifred E. Howe's management. The close, detailed scrutiny she gave to every stage of publication — from copy to the last proof — represented editorial standards seldom exceeded.

The DINNER

Given by the Truftees of

THE METROPOLITAN MUSEUM OF ART

On the Occafion of the Opening

OF

The American Wing

At the University Club

FIFTH AVENUE AND 54TH STREET

NOVEMBER 10, 1924

A menu, 6 x 9 inches, printed at The Museum Press for a
memorable occasion.

THE GREETINGS OF THE SEA-
SON FROM THE TRUSTEES
OF THE METROPOLITAN MU-
SEUM OF ART, MCMXXIII

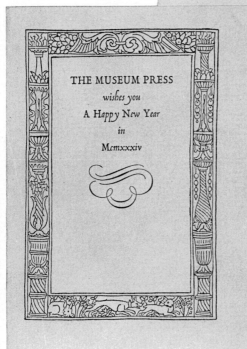

THE MUSEUM PRESS
wishes you
A Happy New Year
in
Mcmxxxiv

Four of the Christmas Greetings designed by Mr. Kent
and printed at The Museum
Press.

This, in Arrighi and Centaur Types,
is sent to The Friends
of
The Museum Press

WITH
CHRISTMAS
GREET·
INGS
AN·
DOMINI
MCM
XX
VI

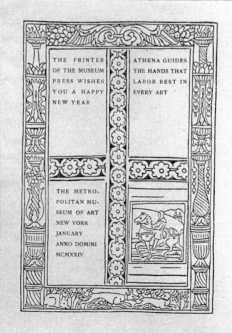

THE PRINTER
OF THE MUSEUM
PRESS WISHES
YOU A HAPPY
NEW YEAR

ATHENA GUIDES
THE HANDS THAT
LABOR BEST IN
EVERY ART

THE METRO·
POLITAN MU·
SEUM OF ART
NEW YORK
JANUARY
ANNO DOMINI
MCMXXIV

TO THE EMPLOYING PRINTERS ON
THE OCCASION OF THEIR VISIT TO THE
METROPOLITAN MUSEUM OF ART, NEW
YORK, OCTOBER V. MCMXIV, THIS LOCUS
CLASSICUS OF PRINTING, DONE AT THE
MUSEUM PRESS WITH CENTAUR TYPES
DESIGNED BY BRUCE ROGERS, IS PRESENTED

THE METROPOLITAN MUSEUM OF ART · NEW YORK

VISIT OF THE GARDEN CLUB OF AMERICA · MAY · 1933

Special groups were greeted by these souvenirs designed by Mr. Kent
and printed at The Museum Press. (Considerably reduced.)

The busy front door of the Museum's public relations is the Information and Sales Desk, and as the services offered to the public increased and the number of publications and photographs available grew, and as the need to answer questions became imperative, the work of this division became ever livelier and more complicated. It was well handled by Miss Juliet W. Robinson, whom I brought from Norwich, and then by Miss Evelyn B. Grier. So inevitable does such a department seem, like a telephone switchboard, that it is hard to believe that when I came to the Museum in 1905 neither of these nerve centers existed.

When the Metropolitan Museum was organized, Professor Comfort, one of the Incorporators, who had given careful study to the Victoria and Albert Museum in London, which is devoted to the needs of the practical designer and artist, was responsible for the clause in the Charter which reads: "and the application of arts to manufactures and practical life." The Museum therefore was committed to the service of this class, although little had been done to carry out the duty in the early period, partly because Industry did not demand or even ask it.

I had grown up in the last half of the nineteenth century, and like all young people interested in the study of the arts of design, I was greatly influenced by what went on in England during that time, the beginning and the establishment of the Machine Age. It would be difficult for one who did not see the changes that took place then to understand the full meaning of the revolution, especially in its effect upon design.

It is a remarkable thing, the antithesis of what might have been expected, that with the machine and the disappearance of the influence of the guilds came better design and a far wider, better, more understanding use of it than had ever happened before.

In France, that land of guilds, designers began to work for the machine soon after its advent, but in this country where the term "machine-made" signified cheap goods and poor design it was a long time before the character of the product changed. William Morris, Ruskin, and, later, the Arts and Crafts Societies, whether they meant to or not, helped to bring about this change.

Once, while in London, I went by accident to a meeting of the Society for the Protection of Ancient Buildings, which was held in a lovely old building in the Inns of Court that I wanted to draw. The presiding officer, a gentleman in tweeds with a buckthorn stick, apologized for taking the chair in the place of the noble lord who was advertised to act as chairman. He was so amusing in his remarks on the address of the day about the monuments in St. Paul's, which he said he would throw into the underground, that I asked who the gentleman was. I was rebuked by a reporter for not knowing that it was William Morris, my long-time beau ideal. I determined to speak to him, and to make my doing so reasonable, I asked him what one did to become a member of the Society. He replied, "You pay your guinea, young man, that's all we want of you." With great glee I told this to Cyril Davenport, Curator of Gems, Medals and Coins in the British Museum, once when I was lunching with him, and his reply was, "William Morris, oh yes, you mean the man who makes wallpaper that no gentleman uses."

Coming to New York's museum of art led me to think of what I had learned of such museums in my first and later European trips. Many of them were, to be sure, old-fashioned museums, that is, collections of works of art open to visitors, but there were those influenced by Bode through his new classification of these arts, or by the museums like those in Switzerland and Munich which had adopted a new method of presentation of their collections, or, of course, the Victoria and Albert Museum, which was avowedly organized to help develop and improve English industry. Norwich had taught me the importance of help to the industries as well as to the people. In the manufacture of textiles there the need for improvement in the artistic quality of their products was patent, and the training of designers to do this work was one of the things the Academy sought to provide. So the intent of the Metropolitan's Charter was clear, and led to our undertaking to provide the opportunity for New York manufacturers to make themselves independent of European houses in the matter of design. It was during the first World War, when manufacturers in this country were cut off from their customary sources of design in Europe, that the help the Museum might offer became of real importance. Our efforts found sympathetic assistance from some of the city's most prominent and influential manufacturers, notably the members of the Art-in-Trades Club. This club, organized in 1906, was

155

composed of men who were engaged in or interested in the arts and art trades; its purpose was the study of the principles of art as applied to trades connected with the decoration and furnishing of buildings. Mr. William Sloane Coffin, afterwards President of the Museum, was active in this organization, and so was Harry Wearne. The members met frequently in the Museum and helped greatly in its attempts to "make the galleries work," especially in many of its fifteen exhibitions of industrial art.

My friend Professor Charles R. Richards, who was, at various times, Director of Cooper Union, Director of the American Association of Museums, Director of the Division of Industrial Art of the General Education Board, chairman of a commission appointed by the Secretary of Commerce to report on the International Exposition of Decorative Arts held in Paris in 1925, and Executive Vice-President of the Museum of Science and Industry, was the most influential exponent of industrial design in America. His books on the subject alone, *Art in Industry* (1922), *The Industrial Museum* (1925), and *Industrial Art and the Museum* (1927), gave him that distinction. His association with the Museum in its exhibitions of art in industry and in all its attempts to promote interest in this subject was of the greatest value.

My efforts to help manufacturers and designers were greatly strengthened by the appointment of Richard F. Bach, Curator of the School of Architecture of Columbia University, as Associate in Industrial Arts. The
156 Metropolitan Museum *Bulletin* for September, 1918,[2]

states, "Mr. Bach will devote himself to the needs of manufacturers, dealers, designers, artisans, and manual craftsmen in objects of industrial art." This he did with great success, and he made his office, as it was hoped he would, a veritable clearing house for all who desired to make practical use of the Museum collections. He helped with the industrial art exhibitions, not alone as a Museum official but also as a most friendly member of the Art-in-Trades Club. He helped in upholding my hands in our endeavors, and also in his own thoroughgoing understanding of what we were trying to do.

The efforts we made to interest people in using the Museum found wide appreciation. An article written by R. L. Duffus called "The Museum Takes Off Its High Hat," which appeared in the *North American Review* in the autumn issue of 1936, summed up the whole matter:[3]

"Mr. Kent divides museum functions into three parts. The first is acquisition. When the Met builds an American Wing and stocks it . . . that is acquisition. The second is exhibition, which is putting things out where people can see them conveniently and to good advantage. This is old stuff. . . . But the third function is exposition — trying to get people to see what the exhibits mean, giving them a chance to use them, apply them in their businesses or professions, work them into their daily lives. That is new.

"To be precise, it is not so much new in theory as in fact. . . .

"It took a long time, but about 1905 the answer

seemed to come. The Met was to be a kind of laboratory — a kind of cultural clinic, if you like. . . . In 1907 Mr. Kent was made Supervisor of Museum Instruction, and the fun began.

"There are a few landmarks that give the idea of what happened: school teachers and pupils invited to come in small groups, 1905; a lending collection of magic lantern slides, 1907; first lectures for salespeople, 1914; first exhibit of industrial art, 1917; first production of educational motion pictures by the museum, 1922. The museum was coming out of its brick-and-stone shell. It was putting its collections to work. It was making people see what the past has to do with the present: not the past of books, which are sometimes hard to read, but the past of the things books tell about, with the brush marks, scars of the chisel, toolings, weavings and embroideries of patient, long-vanished fingers still visible."

Thank you, Mr. Duffus, you helped us a lot.

The things we did have now become a part of the equipment of the Museum for its work with those practical people, the manufacturers and their designers, and have served the country well, especially during the war years.

Our experience in turning the Museum into an educational agency was most exhilarating for those who were doing the planning and the work. We showed, as Mr. Duffus points out, that a museum need not be just a peep show for the curious or a place for students of the history of art to do their studying in, but

158 might be a really practical place for the artists and

designers of the future to see what others of their various arts and crafts have done and to learn how to make these same things fit into our modern life and needs. This, of course, was what the writers of the Charter intended should be done. This is exactly what Ruskin and William Morris in England wanted, what in the Machine Age people were puzzled about, and what it seemed to some of us a museum of art should teach its public. I remember, once, being puzzled by the changes that were taking place in printing when the machines of one kind and another were usurping old methods using the hand of man. I asked Theodore De Vinne, the great American printer, what the result would be, and his reply was, "I leave that all to you young men, but don't forget that the machine is run, like the hand of man, by the brain behind it."

Today, when everything is done by the machine, nobody ever thinks of what would have happened to us if the machine had not taken its place as the recognized power in the world for making and doing things. Looking back, it is interesting to see what this quiet revolution has done already to the industrial arts and, looking forward, it is interesting to speculate on what will be the result for the museums of the future, those, at least, that collect the arts of design. The arts made by the hands of Egyptian, Greek, Roman, and all the rest of the ancient world will be shown side by side with those of today done by the machine. In this connection, it may be remembered that Professor Whitehead says: "Nothing does more harm in unnerving men for their duties in the present, than the attention devoted to the points of excellence in the past as compared with the average failure of the present day."[4] The answer is, there need be no exhibition of the failures, the museum may see to this in its selection of examples.

I have already told in Chapter VI how my acquaintance in Norwich with American furniture, silver, etc., and with collectors of these things brought about the inclusion of an American section in the Hudson-Fulton exhibition. Soon after the exhibition, Eugene Bolles told me of his desire to sell his collection, which consisted chiefly of seventeenth-century furniture, and I promptly reported the opportunity to Mr. de Forest. To emphasize the importance of the collection to the Museum, I invited Mr. and Mrs. de Forest and R. T. H. Halsey to go with me as my guests to Boston, where we would see what Boston and its vicinity had to show of American arts and crafts. We went, and had dinner at the Copley-Plaza Hotel, to which I had invited Hollis French, Joseph Chandler, Sumner Appleton, prominent collectors of American things, to meet my friends. The next day we motored to Salem, and then to Danvers, Topsfield, and Beverly; we devoted our attention to seventeenth-century buildings and other things, saw the Essex Institute, the Rebecca Nurse house, the Parson Capen house, and lunched with Charles Tyler and had a real fish chowder, which these New Yorkers had never eaten before. Back in Boston I showed them Christ Church, the Paul Revere house, and the old State House. Then we came home, I think with my purpose already accomplished, namely, to emphasize

the importance of showing the history of American objects in an American museum. The Bolles collection was forthwith purchased for the Museum by a gift of Mrs. Russell Sage, and it became the nucleus which in time developed into the American Wing.

The purchase of the Bolles collection in 1909 was the occasion for the founding of the Walpole Society, a group of the most distinguished first collectors of American things — furniture, silver, and what not. It came about in this way. Luke Vincent Lockwood, who had written a book on American furniture, and I went on to Boston to conclude the transaction with Bolles, and we handed him his check in the Union Club over a magnum of champagne. Realizing how few collectors of such things at that time knew one another, I proposed the organization of a society so that they might come together, which met with the approval of the others, and we immediately took the necessary steps to bring this about. The first meeting was held in Hartford on January 21, 1910, with twelve gentlemen present, and the group has gone on with enthusiasm ever since, till now, with all the losses by death since then, there are twenty-eight men who are loyal to the Society.

Among the men who have been members are such distinguished collectors as Edwin A. Barber of Philadelphia, Richard A. Canfield and Charles A. Munn of New York, George S. Palmer of New London, Marsden J. Perry of Providence, Albert H. Pitkin of Hartford, Charles H. Tyler and Dwight Blaney of Boston, George F. Dow of Salem, Henry Wood Erving of Hartford, R. T. Haines Halsey of New York, Norman M. Isham of Providence, and Harry Harkness Flagler of New York. 161

The club was named for Horace Walpole, fourth earl of Orford, who did in his way what we were to try to do, make the arts of his country better known through his collecting and writing. Meetings are held once or twice a year; at each meeting a different locality is visited, and the buildings and collections of those places are studied. A "Note Book" is issued, with articles and notes on what was seen, well printed as Walpole would have done at Strawberry Hill.

It is interesting to observe a certain fact about collections of objects of art made by real collectors, that eventually, like collections of books, they come into public museums or libraries. That was true of the collections of all the members of the Walpole Society who are no longer living.

I don't think there is any reason now for not remembering, and telling, what happened when the American Wing was first planned. The Director was not interested in, certainly not enthusiastic about, the showing of these American things, feeling as he did that they were not really worthy of the Museum, were not in the class with Greek and Egyptian art. He consulted with his Boston Museum friends, who also felt as he did that the American arts and crafts were not worthy of exhibition. However, a few years later, his article in the pamphlet[5] announcing the gift of the Wing by Mr. and Mrs. de Forest admitted the importance of American art for Americans, the fact that our earlier "builders and craftsmen were endowed with a fine sense of line, proportion, and the proper limits of decoration," and that "their work is never vulgar."

The great success of these things when shown the public in the Hudson-Fulton exhibition and the American Wing, together with Charles Tyler's bequest to the Boston Museum, led Boston to change its mind eventually, Heaven be praised.

The building of additions to the Museum has always interested me. Museum buildings in this country were done usually by architects in the old Beaux-Arts school manner, with little thought for museum contents and their needs. John Dana was right in his strictures on this kind of building, in his article, "The Museum in the Park." His proposal of movable partitions was a good suggestion to builders, especially of small museums.

The American Wing in particular presented interesting problems to be solved. There was first of all the problem of the arrangement of whole rooms, with their woodwork intact, in proper sequence and relationship. We had as models the German and Swiss museums, especially the one at Zurich, where planning by architects had given way to planning by curators. Our chief concern was the fitting into a given floor space of the seventeenth-, eighteenth-, and early nineteenth-century rooms that we had to show, which required what might be called a "loft building," the fenestration to fit the needs of the rooms, not the architect's idea of how such apertures should look in his façade.

I drew the first sketch plans for the building, and Durr Friedley, then Acting Curator of the European and American decorative arts, did a detailed set. In the planning we had the advice and help of my friends 163

Norman Isham, George Francis Dow, and other Walpolians who were wise in the matters of early architecture and crafts. The Museum architects, McKim, Mead & White, declined the job, and Mr. de Forest asked his friend Grosvenor Atterbury to take it on, which he did. R. T. Haines Halsey on becoming a Trustee was immediately appointed Chairman of the Committee on American Decorative Art. For a year before the American Wing was opened he devoted all his time to the details of its installation. A few years earlier when the old Assay Office on Wall Street was being torn down, Mr. de Forest had arranged for its façade to be given to the Museum. This was used as the façade to the Wing, opening on the court, which was turned into a garden in the old American style, with box and shrubs, and, set in the paving, millstones from Connecticut.

The opening of the American Wing, like the Hudson-Fulton exhibition, astonished everybody by the interest and attendance it attracted. Those of us of the staff who had worked hard to bring it about were well repaid. American decorative art had suddenly been put on the map.

An earlier opportunity to help with the planning of museum architecture had come to me in 1912, through the invitation of the President of the newly organized Cleveland Museum of Art to act as adviser to its Building Committee — a most delightful experience which I owe also to the liberality of my own Trustees who permitted me to accept the invitation. Plans for the building to be erected in Wade Park had been drawn by the local architects, Messrs. Hubbell & Benes, who had made a very good job of it, but I was able to suggest certain additions and subtractions which I had learned about by practical administrative experience, to allow for offices, storage rooms, and things like that which architects are not interested in. The Museum was opened in June, 1916. After the building was erected, I was asked to help in the purchase of its collections, in the planning of its *Bulletin,* and other details.

During the years that I was employed at the Metropolitan Museum there grew up associations like the American Association of Museums, organized in 1906, composed of and run entirely by museum-employed people, and the American Federation of Arts, organized by Elihu Root, Robert de Forest, and others in 1909, and run by Miss Leila Mechlin. I had a part in these two associations, on their boards and various committees. They did much for the extension of knowledge of museum management, for co-operation between museums, and for the education of people about to enter the museum field. Classes were formed for such people at Harvard's Fogg Museum, by John Dana in the Newark Museum, and afterwards in other places. Sometimes confusion existed in such schools, education in the history of art being mistaken for the necessary education in museum economy, as Dewey would have called it. I see now why Dewey in his lectures to students in the Library School did not waste his time on the character of the literature in his books, but devoted himself to the "economy" side of his subject, leaving the other sort of lectures to the professors of the colleges.

At one time and another, while I was at the Metropolitan, I was sounded out regarding my acceptance of the directorship of the Boston Museum if offered, and was offered the directorship of the museums of Philadelphia, Buffalo, Indianapolis, and Cleveland, also the librarianship of Williams College; but I found my chief interest lay in New York, and so I stayed there until my working days were over.

In 1932, I was given an assistant to help me in my work, Lauder Greenway, a Yale graduate who had a term, also, at Cambridge University, one who gave promise of real helpfulness and ever fulfilled that assurance. I kept him waiting too long, but when I retired in 1940, he succeeded to the secretaryship, for which he was well fitted.

And now, my museum employment having come to an end, I cannot but wonder whether my "education" really fitted me for what I undertook to do — whether I could have learned more if I had gone to college and whether I accomplished anything or not.

In 1920 Hamilton College gave me an honorary Master's degree, and in 1932 Brown University made me an honorary Doctor of Art, both honors that made me feel that I had, perhaps, really appeared to have educated myself for my museum work. The Hamilton degree came during the Honorable Elihu Root's presidency of the college and was valued the more because of his interest. The Brown degree was given, I believe, partly in recognition of my long service to the two or-

166

ganizations in which Frederick P. Keppel had so great an interest, the Museums Association and the Federation of Arts, and to which he had given so generously of Carnegie Corporation funds. My membership on Mr. Keppel's committee of the Carnegie Corporation was helpful to him, I hope, in his service to these organizations.

I cannot help wondering also whether museums themselves have made good in their attempts to prove that they are an important educational factor in this country, along with the schools and libraries. Perhaps it is too soon to try to answer this question, perhaps we must leave it to the student of educational work to give the answer in the years to come. That the museums have grown rich in their collections we will admit, but are our people more understanding of the value and the power of art? Are there signs of our becoming an art-loving, art-producing people?

The museum when it was founded in this country was looked upon as an ornament to the city, a place for people who were curious about what was in it to go, and to take their friends. The British Museum had taught us that there were scholars who would want to use it as a place for study, but in America these were few and far between. The thing our museums should do is to teach people the value of art, using the things in the museum to point the moral. Alfred North Whitehead in his *Aims of Education*[6] has well expressed what seems to me the real purpose of American museums:

"Finally, there should grow the most austere of all   167

mental qualities; I mean the sense for style. It is an aesthetic sense, based on admiration for the direct attainment of a foreseen end, simply and without waste. Style in art, style in literature, style in science, style in logic, style in practical execution have fundamentally the same aesthetic qualities, namely, attainment and restraint. . . .

"Style, in its finest sense, is the last acquirement of the educated mind; it is also the most useful. It pervades the whole being. . . . Style is the ultimate morality of mind."

NOTES

[1] *Paragraphs on Printing Elicited from Bruce Rogers in Talks with James Hendrickson on the Functions of the Book Designer,* New York: William E. Rudge's Sons, 1943, p. 27.

[2] Vol. 13, p. 208.

[3] Vol. 242, pp. 34-44.

[4] Alfred North Whitehead, *Science and the Modern World: Lowell Lectures, 1925,* New York: The Macmillan Company, 1926, p. 294.

[5] *An American Wing for The Metropolitan Museum of Art: The Gift of Robert W. de Forest and Emily Johnston de Forest. Bulletin of The Metropolitan Museum of Art,* November, 1922, Part II.

[6] *The Aims of Education & Other Essays,* New York: The Macmillan Company, 1929, p. 19.

THE PUBLISHED

WRITINGS OF

HENRY WATSON KENT

WHEN THE INCLUSION of a list of Mr. Kent's writings in this volume of his memoirs was broached, he demurred, insisting that he was not an author and that what he had written was not important. Nevertheless, the Committee on Publications of The Grolier Club, and other of Mr. Kent's friends, believed such a list valuable, and the Committee therefore assumed responsibility for its inclusion. In it may be found a suggestion of interests and activities neglected or given short shrift in the reticent and highly selective memoirs, as well as record of the preoccupations more fully narrated there. And if the material here listed be read, there emerges a commentary on the part of reading in this education, and, likewise, the presence of a prose style of distinction — the distinction that comes from reading insistently and curiously, professionally, too, but at the same time in the spirit of the true amateur, to savor and to enjoy.

What to include in the list presented problems. The tradition of anonymity, in the Slater Memorial Museum, in The Grolier Club, in the Metropolitan Museum, was strong — whether initiated or merely reinforced by Mr. Kent I cannot say. It is characteristic, for example, that the pamphlet *Furniture . . . and Various Devices Used in the Museum* (see above, p. 93) nowhere bears his name and is not catalogued as his in the Metropolitan Museum Library. For the Slater Museum and Peck Library catalogues, sometimes only lists, I have assumed that during Mr. Kent's time they might with reasonable safety be attributed to him. Some of them are mentioned in his text, as indicated by the "See above" references. It is much to be regretted, of course, that he did not check the assembled list. For The Grolier Club catalogues, happily, I have the assurance of having gone over a list of them with Mr. Kent in 1947, and of having noted down where he considered himself author and where editor. I had also two written communications from him listing Grolier Club publications of his authorship.

At the Metropolitan Museum, the problem of attribution is vastly more complicated. From 1905 until his retirement at the end of 1940, Mr. Kent was in effect, though not so called, director of publications. In this sense, he might be called editor of all Museum publications during that period. But this list is intended to record authorship and editorship in the more limited sense, and for the larger part of this period the Museum had its Editor of Publications and, from 1924, a growing editorial staff. Of all the publications, then, little and big, that passed through his hands and under his eye, which ones should be attributed to his editorship, which to his authorship? The lines between literary editorship and typographical design accompanied by lively interest in content, between conception and actual compilation, which seem distinct in the abstract, tend to blur as one thinks back over actual publica-

tions. Roughly, it might be said that the publications covering the collections and exhibitions — catalogues and the like — were not of Mr. Kent's authorship or editorship, though consigned to him for production and sale. Exceptions are two or three of the catalogues in the American field, and perhaps he should be considered editor of the series of *Picture Books*, pamphlets with some twenty full-page illustrations and a brief introductory text, designed to sell at popular prices and meet a popular need — an idea he brought back from one of the English museums. Almost always of Mr. Kent's conception and direction, on the other hand, are publications interpreting the ways and works of the Museum to the public, including, certainly until 1925 when it passed from his personal supervision, the educational work. Announcements of lectures, cinema films, lending collections; information concerning membership; the *Weekly Calendar of Events* (October, 1925 — December, 1940); special Museum anniversaries; lists of publications and reproductions — from one point of view these are the ephemera of Museum life; from another, they become suggestive indices of a growing educational service, an expanding publications program, and a mind active to set these things forth attractively. Of the many folders frequently reprinted under varying titles and in changing formats, I have selected five for listing as representative: one almost certainly of Mr. Kent's personal compiling, the little type specimen book, and four of his editorship — three concerning publications, *Publications on Sale*, *Reproductions on Sale* (the *Cyclopedia*), and *Christmas Suggestions*, and one summarizing Museum services, hours, etc., the *Dictionary*, first called *What The Metropolitan Museum of Art Is Doing*.

Of the contributions to periodicals and newspapers

listed, most are signed or initialed. It is characteristic that *Business Methods in The Metropolitan Museum of Art,* the record of Mr. Kent's great achievement in organizing the administrative routine of the Museum, which was published in the *Proceedings of the American Association of Museums* with his name, should have appeared with no hint of authorship in the Museum's *Bulletin* of August, 1911. Signed articles by him in the *Bulletin* are few — the first in 1910; we may suppose that many more articles and notes from his pen were published there, especially in the early years when the staff was small, but there is no way of identifying them now.

I have much help to acknowledge, for, looking back, I am aware how little a bibliographer works alone. A copy of a list of Mr. Kent's writings, of which typescripts exist in several places, was made for me through the kindness of Mr. Walter Hauser, Librarian of The Metropolitan Museum of Art; I am under obligation to this unknown predecessor, whose identity I have tried in vain to discover.

For friendly courtesies facilitating my examination of publications of the Norwich Free Academy and the Slater Memorial Museum I am indebted to Mrs. Charlotte Eastman, former Director of the Art School, to Mrs. Ozias Dodge, the present Curator of the Museum, and to Miss Elizabeth E. Bean, Librarian of the Peck Library. Miss Louise Lockridge, Assistant to the Director of the George Walter Smith Art Museum of the City Library Association, Springfield, Massachusetts, and Miss Alice W. Kendall, Director of the Newark Museum, contributed much information about publications resulting from Mr. Kent's association with John Cotton Dana. Miss Blanche Decker, Executive Secretary of the American Institute of Graphic

Arts, assisted greatly with details of Mr. Kent's writing for the Institute. Mr. George L. McKay, Librarian of The Grolier Club, helped all along the line, as well as with the Club's own books and periodicals.

For the Metropolitan Museum publications, I had not only my own recollection of procedure to draw on, but also the thoughtful appraisals of Miss Winifred E. Howe, the Museum's former Editor of Publications, so closely associated with Mr. Kent in all work on publications for thirty of his thirty-five years there. The list of Museum publications by years, compiled by Mr. A. T. Gardner, Research Fellow, was an assistance. I am grateful, too, for much patient and interested help on all kinds of details from members of the Museum staff, many of whom had served under Mr. Kent's direction.

After Mr. Kent's death, his nephew, Mr. Richard Kent, extended to me the great privilege of access to his uncle's books and papers, while they were still in the careful order in which their owner had left them. My examination of them answered some questions and raised others, for example, as to whether a number of addresses of which I found copies might have been published in some form that had not come to my attention. In this connection, and in others, many associations, libraries, and individuals courteously and promptly answered inquiries and checked details.

Indispensable to every bibliographer, editor, and research worker in Philadelphia is the Union Library Catalogue and its unfailingly helpful staff. Like so many indispensables, this service has come to be taken for granted but, remembering the days when it did not exist, I should like to record my lively appreciation.

173

These many individuals, named and unnamed, furthered the completeness and accuracy of this list of Mr. Kent's writings. But without Mr. Lauder Greenway, formerly Secretary of The Metropolitan Museum and now Vice-Chairman of the Institute of Fine Arts of New York University, there would have been no list. In acknowledging so complete an indebtedness I can only say, gratefully, "Here, thanks to you, the list is."

LOIS LEIGHTON COMINGS

Books and Pamphlets Written or Compiled by Henry Watson Kent

1

Norwich Free Academy. Catalogue and Brief Description of the Plaster Reproductions of Greek and Italian Sculpture in the Slater Memorial Museum, Norwich, Conn. Cambridge, Mass.: John Wilson and Son, University Press, 1889.

Introductory Note signed "R[obert] P[orter] K[eep]" says, "... the present guide to the Sculptures has been compiled by Mr. H. W. Kent, the Curator of the Museum."

2

Exhibition of Paintings Loaned by Mr. W. A. Slater. Norwich, Conn.: Slater Memorial Museum, January 22, 1890.

Unsigned. See above, p. 58.
Reprinted in 1891.

3

Exhibition of Paintings Loaned by Mr. W. A. Slater. Norwich, Conn.: Slater Memorial Museum, January 13, 1891.

Reprint of the pamphlet of 1890.

4

Catalogue of an Exhibition to Illustrate the Effect of Color in Greek Sculpture, June, 1892. [Norwich, Conn.]: Slater Memorial Museum, 1892.

5

Exhibition of Paintings Loaned by Mr. W. A. Slater, June, 1894. [Norwich, Conn.]: Slater Memorial Museum, 1894.

See above, p. 58.
Two editions: one of eight pages, headed "Slater Memorial Museum," with a seal on the next line; the other of four pages, with "Norwich, Conn." replacing the seal.

6

Five Tapestries Loaned by Mr. W. A. Slater, September, 1894. Norwich, Conn.: Slater Memorial Museum, 1894.

7

Catalogue of the Peck Library: Philosophy. [Norwich, Conn.]: Norwich Free Academy, November, 1894.

Twenty-five copies printed.

8

An Exhibition of Bookbindings, December, 1894. Norwich, Conn.: Slater Memorial Museum, 1894.

See above, p. 59.

9

Loan Exhibition of Portraits of Men and Women Connected with the Early History of Norwich, February 22, 1895. Norwich, Conn.: Slater Memorial Museum, 1895.

10

An Exhibition of Water-Colors by Mr. Frank Edward Johnson, November, 1897. Norwich, Conn.: Slater Memorial Museum, 1897.

11

Catalogue of an Exhibition of the Works of Edith Woodman Burroughs, Bryson Burroughs, Ozias Dodge and Bela Lyon Pratt in Sculpture and Painting. Norwich, Conn.: Slater Memorial Museum, November 8 to 15, 1899.

12

The Horace Smith Collection of Casts of Greek and Renaissance Sculpture: A Brief Statement of the Cost and Manner of Its Installation. By Henry Watson Kent. Springfield, Mass.: The City Library Association, January, 1900.

See above, pp. 104-105.

A Tentative Scheme of Classification for the Library of The
Grolier Club. New York: The Grolier Club, 1901.

See above, p. 120.

Reprinted from *Grolier Club Year Book*, 1901. Revised edition, *The Classification Used in the Library of The Grolier Club*, 1910.

Books and
Pamphlets
Written or
Compiled by
H. W. Kent

An Exhibition of Selected Works of the Poets Laureate of England, Exhibited at The Grolier Club from January 25 to February 16, 1901. [New York: The Grolier Club, 1901].

See above, pp. 120-121.

Catalogue of an Exhibition of Selected Works of the Poets Laureate of England. New York: The Grolier Club, 1901.

A revised and corrected edition, on large paper, of the preceding item.

Mosaic Bookbindings: A Catalogue of an Exhibition. New York: The Grolier Club, January 23 to February 22, 1902.

See above, p. 121.

Bibliographical Notes on One Hundred Books Famous in English Literature. Compiled by Henry W. Kent. New York: The Grolier Club, 1903.

See above, p. 121.

Exhibition of Silver, Embroidered, and Curious Bookbindings. New York: The Grolier Club, April 16 to May 9, 1903.

See above, p. 121.

Catalogue of Books, Engravings, Water-Colors, & Sketches by William Blake, Exhibited at The Grolier Club from January 26 to February 25, MCMV. [New York: The Grolier Club, 1905].

See above, p. 121. "The [Blake] exhibition was arranged by Henry W. Kent, who made the catalogue, by far the most extensive up to that time on the subject."—Ruth Shepard Granniss, *The Grolier Club and Its Exhibitions*, New York: The Grolier Club, 1944, pp. 21-22.

20

176 Catalogue of Ornamental Leather Bookbindings Executed in

America Prior to 1850, Exhibited at The Grolier Club, November 7 to 30, 1907. [New York: The Grolier Club, 1907].

21

Catalogue of an Exhibition of American Paintings, Furniture, Silver, and Other Objects of Art, MDCXXV-MDCCCXXV. By Henry Watson Kent and Florence N. Levy. The Hudson-Fulton Celebration, Catalogue of an Exhibition Held in The Metropolitan Museum of Art, vol. II. New York: [The Metropolitan Museum of Art], 1909.

22

Sample Book of Printing Types, with a Note on the Preparation of Copy for Labels. New York: The Metropolitan Museum of Art, 1909.

In the earlier list of Mr. Kent's work, but I have not seen a copy and it is not in Mr. Gardner's bibliography of Museum publications. Revised editions in 1912 and, as *Printing Types Used by the Museum Press,* in 1926 and 1934.

23

The Classification Used in the Library of The Grolier Club. New York: The Grolier Club, 1910.

See above, p. 120.
Revised edition of *A Tentative Scheme of Classification . . .,* 1901. Reprinted from *Grolier Club Year Book,* 1910.

24

Sample Book of Printing Types, with a Note on the Preparation of Labels. [New York]: The Metropolitan Museum of Art, 1912.

Revision of the edition of 1909. Subsequent editions as *Printing Types Used by the Museum Press* in 1926 and 1934.

25

To the Committee on Educational Work [report of educational work of the Museum for the year 1916]. [New York]: The Metropolitan Museum of Art, [1917].

Signed at the end "Henry W. Kent, Secretary" and dated January 10, 1917.

26

To the Committee on Educational Work [report of educational work of the Museum for the year 1919]. New York: The Metropolitan Museum of Art, 1919.

Signed at the end "H. W. Kent, Secretary." Dated at the beginning November 5, 1919.

27

Report to the Committee on Educational Work [report of educational work of the Museum for the year 1922]. [New York]: The Metropolitan Museum of Art, [1922].

Signed at the end "H. W. Kent, Secretary" and dated November 29, 1922.

28

Drawings and Measurements of Furniture Used by the Museum. New York: The Metropolitan Museum of Art, 1923.

Unsigned. See above, p. 93.
Reprinted in expanded form as *Furniture, with Drawings & Measurements, and Various Devices Used by the Museum,* 1930.

29

Printing Types Used by the Museum Press. New York: The Metropolitan Museum of Art, 1926.

Revised edition of *Sample Book of Printing Types,* 1909 and 1912. Later revision, 1934.

30

Some Business Methods Used in the Museum. By Henry W. Kent, Secretary. [New York]: The Metropolitan Museum of Art, 1926.

See above, pp. 141-142.
Reprinted from *Proceedings of the American Association of Museums,* 1911.

31

The Fifth Passport Printed by Benjamin Franklin at his Passy Press. New York: Printed for Watson Kent, 1927.

32

Furniture, with Drawings & Measurements, and Various Devices Used by the Museum. New York: The Metropolitan Museum of Art, 1930.

Unsigned. See above, p. 93.
Reprint, in expanded form, of *Drawings and Measurements of Furniture Used by the Museum,* 1923.

33

Printing Types Used by the Museum Press. New York: The Metropolitan Museum of Art, 1934.

Revision of the pamphlet of 1926. Earlier editions as *Sample Book of*

Printing Types in 1909 and 1912. Note on "The Preparation of Copy for Labels" omitted.

34

St. Distaff's Day: An Address by Henry W. Kent on the occasion of a dinner given by the women engaged in the making of books. White Plains, N. Y.: The Froben Press, 1938. American Institute of Graphic Arts Keepsake No. 57.

35

Henry Walters, 1848-1931. By Henry Watson Kent. An Address in Baltimore, January Twenty-seventh, Walters Art Gallery, Baltimore, Maryland, 1940. n.p., n.d.

36

50 Books of the Year 1942. n.p., [1942]. American Institute of Graphic Arts Keepsake No. 69.

Also printed in *Print,* Spring, 1942.

37

The Grolier Club and Its Iconographic Collections: An Address by Henry Watson Kent, November 18, 1943. New York: The Grolier Club, 1944.

38

Address by H. W. Kent on the Occasion of the Unveiling of a Tablet in Memory of William Clifford Erected by The Metropolitan Museum Employees' Association October 16, 1944. n.p., n.d.

Contributions by Henry Watson Kent
to Books and Pamphlets

39

Map of Norwich as in 1705 *and* Plan of Pews in Church about 1756 [drawings]. *In* Old Houses of the Antient Town of Norwich, 1660-1800, by Mary E. Perkins, pp. 104, 352. Norwich, Conn., 1895.

See above, p. 81.

40

Introductory Note. *In* A Brief Outline of the History of Libraries, by Justus Lipsius, translated from the second edition (Antwerp, The Plantin Press, John Moretus, 1607), the last from the hand of the author, by John Cotton Dana, pp. 9-20. Literature of Libraries in the Seventeenth and Eighteenth Centuries, edited by John Cotton Dana and Henry W. Kent, No. 5. Chicago, Ill.: A. C. McClurg & Co., 1907.

See above, pp. 118-119.

41

[Letter from Robert Restieaux on Cardelius]. *In* Who Was Cardelius? edited by John Cotton Dana, pp. 7-8. Cambridge, Mass.: The University Press, 1909. Issued by The Printing Art.

See above, pp. 119-120.
Reprinted from the *Nation*, May 6, 1909.

42

Introductory Note. *In* Essay on Bibliography and on the Attainments of a Librarian, by Parent the Elder, translated by Mrs. Schuyler Van Rensselaer, pp. iii-vii. The Librarian's Series, edited by John Cotton Dana and Henry W. Kent, No. 4. Woodstock, Vt.: The Elm Tree Press, 1914.

See above, p. 119.

43

The Spencer Collection. *In* The Spencer Collection of Modern Book Bindings, pp. 3-7. New York: The New York Public Library, 1914.

See above, pp. 127-128.
Reprinted from the article in *Bulletin of The New York Public Library*, June, 1914. Reprinted also in the revised edition, *The Spencer Collection of Illustrated Books*, 1928.

44

The Publications. *In* Transactions of The Grolier Club of the City of New York: From July eighteen hundred and ninety-nine to December nineteen hundred and nineteen, Part IV, pp. 69-78. New York: The Grolier Club, 1921.

45

Chez Moreau de Saint-Méry, Philadelphie. With a List of Imprints enlarged by George Parker Winship. *In* Bibliographical Essays: A Tribute to Wilberforce Eames, pp. 66-78. [Cambridge, Mass.: Harvard University Press], 1924.

Address. *In* Addresses on the Occasion of the Opening of the American Wing, pp. 22-29. New York: The Metropolitan Museum of Art, 1925.

Objects of Art in Color Reproductions. *In* Achievement in Photo-Engraving and Letter-Press Printing, 1927, compiled and edited by Louis Flader, pp. 65-66. Chicago, Ill.: American Photo-Engravers Association, [cop. 1927].

The Spencer Collection. *In* The Spencer Collection of Illustrated Books, pp. vii-xi. New York: The New York Public Library, 1928.

Revised edition of *The Spencer Collection of Modern Book Bindings,* 1914.

The Museum and Industrial Art. *In* Art in Industry: Being the Report of an Industrial Art Survey Conducted under the Auspices of The National Society for Vocational Education and the Department of Education of the State of New York, by Charles R. Richards, pp. 435-439. New York: The Macmillan Company, 1929.

Address [on Robert W. de Forest]. *In* Exercises in Memory of Robert W. de Forest, Edward D. Adams, George F. Baker, Charles W. Gould, and Edward Robinson, pp. 14-15. New York: The Metropolitan Museum of Art, 1931.

[Letter on John Cotton Dana], *under* The Museum and American Art. *In* The Newark Museum: A Chronicle of the Founding Years, 1909-1934, pp. 10-11. Newark, N. J., [1934].

Mr. Kent's Address. *In* An Account of the Celebration of John Cotton Dana Day at the Newark Museum, Held under the Sponsorship of the Newark Educational Council, October 6, 1935, pp. 8-10. [Newark]: Published jointly by the Newark Library and the Newark Museum, 1935.

Note. *In* An Exhibition of the Work of Rudolph Ruzicka, [no

181

pagination; note embraces 7 pp.]. New York: The American Institute of Graphic Arts, 1935.

53

The Walpole Society, 1910-1935: A Quarter Century in American Collecting. *In* The Twenty-fifth Anniversary Meeting of The Walpole Society, pp. 11-26. n.p.: Printed by the Society, 1935.

54

[Introduction]. *In* The Fifty Books of the Year: A Cumulative List of the Examples of Bookmaking Selected and Shown by The American Institute of Graphic Arts, [no pagination; introduction embraces 2 pp.]. [New York, 1938]. American Institute of Graphic Arts Keepsake No. 59.

Reprinted from *The Annual of Bookmaking*, 1938.

55

[Address]. *In* Addresses Given at the Opening of the Exhibition of Metropolitan Museum Printing Held in The Pierpont Morgan Library on 24 October 1938, p. 29. New York, 1939. American Institute of Graphic Arts Keepsake No. 58.

See above, pp. 151-152.

56

Preface. *In* The Work of Bruce Rogers, Jack of All Trades, Master of One: A Catalogue of an Exhibition Arranged by The American Institute of Graphic Arts and The Grolier Club of New York, with an Introduction by D. B. Updike, a Letter from John McCutcheon, and an Address by Mr. Rogers, pp. v-vi. New York: Oxford University Press, 1939.

57

Note. *In* Daniel Berkeley Updike and The Merrymount Press, pp. 3-4. New York: The American Institute of Graphic Arts, 1940.

58

Encore Moreau de Saint-Méry. *In* Bookmen's Holiday: Notes and Studies Written and Gathered in Tribute to Harry Miller Lydenberg, pp. 239-247. New York: The New York Public Library, 1943.

59

Remarks of H. W. Kent on the Presentation of the Friedsam Medal, May 2, 1945 [no pagination; remarks cover 2 pp.]. *In*

The Friedsam Medal in Industrial Art, 1945: A Tribute to the
Late Irene Lewisohn. n.p., n.d.

60

B. R.'s Printer's Devices *and* In England. *In* B R Marks & Re-
marks, the Marks by Bruce Rogers, et al., the Remarks by His
Friends: H. W. Kent, J. M. Bowles, Carl Purington Rollins,
David Pottinger, Christopher Morley, James Hendrickson &
Frederic Warde, pp. 1-14, 102-120. New York: The Typophiles,
1946. Typophile Chap Book: XV.

Articles by Henry Watson Kent

in Periodicals and Newspapers

61

School Libraries [letter dated Peck Library, July 22, 1890]. Library Journal, vol. 15, August, 1890, p. 228.

62

A Note from Greece [letter to Dr. Keep from Athens]. Academy
Journal, Norwich, Conn., vol. 4, March, 1893, pp. 5-6.

63

The Selamlik. Academy Journal, Norwich, Conn., vol. 4, April,
1893, pp. 5-7.

64

A Scheme of Classification for the Library. The Grolier Club of
the City of New York: Officers, Committees, Constitution, By-
Laws, House Rules, Members, Annual Reports, etc. [hereafter
called, as commonly, Grolier Club Year Book], 1901, pp. 117-137.
See above, p. 120.
Reprinted as a pamphlet, *A Tentative Scheme of Classification . . .,*
1901. Revised edition, *Grolier Club Year Book,* 1910, and pamphlet,
The Classification Used in the Library of The Grolier Club, 1910.

65

Library Book Plates. Library Journal, vol. 27, November, 1902,
pp. 932-934.

66

A Partial List of Poems on Printing, to be found in the Library.

Grolier Club Year Book, 1903, pp. 127-134.

Not signed, but has been attributed to Mr. Kent, then Librarian of The Grolier Club.

67

Report of the Library Committee. Grolier Club Year Book, 1905, pp. 106-112.

68

[Remarks on educational work and public schools]. Proceedings of the American Association of Museums, vol. 4, 1909, p. 80.

69

Rare Specimens of Gravers' Art: The Society of the Iconophiles Issues a Beautiful Catalogue of Its Privately Engraved Views and Portraits. New York Times, May 1, 1909, Saturday Review of Books, p. 272.

70

A Word about Cardelius [letter signed Robert Restieaux and dated New York, April 15]. Nation, vol. 88, May 6, 1909, p. 461.

See above, pp. 119-120.

Reprinted with other letters on Cardelius in *Who Was Cardelius?* 1909.

71

Classification Used in the Library of The Grolier Club. Grolier Club Year Book, 1910, pp. 123-145.

See above, p. 120.

Revision of *A Scheme of Classification* . . ., 1901. Also reprinted as separate pamphlet, 1910.

72

The Bolles Collection: The Gift of Mrs. Russell Sage. Bulletin of The Metropolitan Museum of Art, vol. 5, January, 1910, pp. 14-16.

73

Art Museums and Schools. Educational Review, vol. 40, June, 1910, pp. 78-81.

74

Librarianship [paper read before the New York Library School]. Library Journal, vol. 35, November, 1910, pp. 483-487.

75

[Remarks on good typography for labels]. Proceedings of the American Association of Museums, vol. 5, 1911, p. 26.

76

Some Business Methods in The Metropolitan Museum of Art. *Ibid.*, pp. 31-34.

See above, pp. 141-142.
Also printed in *Bulletin of The Metropolitan Museum of Art*, August, 1911. Reprinted as pamphlet, *Some Business Methods Used in the Museum*, 1926.

77

The Metropolitan Museum of Art Printing Press. Printing Art, vol. 16, January, 1911, pp. 369-371.

78

Pierre Bayle's Dictionary [paper read before the New York Library Club, November 10, 1910, as a contribution to a "Convention of Books"]. Library Journal, vol. 36, January, 1911, pp. 15-18.

79

Business Methods in The Metropolitan Museum of Art: A Paper Read before the American Association of Museums in Boston, May 23, 1911. Bulletin of The Metropolitan Museum of Art, vol. 6, August, 1911, pp. 169-170.

Unsigned. See above, pp. 141-142. Reprint from *Proceedings of the American Association of Museums*, 1911. Reprinted as pamphlet, *Some Business Methods Used in the Museum*, 1926.

80

Coöperation between Libraries, Schools, and Museums [paper read before the New York State Library Association, September 29, 1911]. Library Journal, vol. 36, November, 1911, pp. 557-560.

81

A Glossary of Art Terms. Proceedings of the American Association of Museums, vol. 6, 1912, pp. 88-90.

82

Librarians' Books [paper read before the New York State Library School, June, 1912]. Library Journal, vol. 37, October, 1912, pp. 550-556.

83

A Book of Sketches by Cellini. Bulletin of The Metropolitan
Museum of Art, vol. 8, February, 1913, pp. 30-31.

84

The Small Museum [paper read at the Fourth Annual Convention of the American Federation of Arts, Washington, D. C.,
May 15 & 16, 1913]. Art and Progress, vol. 4, August, 1913, pp.
1047-1056.

85

The Spencer Collection. Bulletin of The New York Public Library, vol. 18, June, 1914, pp. 533-538.

See above, pp. 127-128.
Reprinted in *The Spencer Collection of Modern Book Bindings,*
1914, and in the revised edition, *The Spencer Collection of Illustrated
Books,* 1928.

86

Address [at the American Library Association Conference, Washington, D. C., May 25-29, 1914, substituting for Mr. Robert W.
de Forest]. Bulletin of the American Library Association, vol.
8, July, 1914, pp. 166-168.

87

The Love of the Book [address at the American Library Association Conference, Berkeley, California, June 3-9, 1915]. Bulletin
of the American Library Association, vol. 9, July, 1915, pp.
94-101.

88

Report of the Committee on Publications. Grolier Club Year
Book, 1916, pp. 111-114.

89

Address at the Formal Dedication of The Cleveland Museum of
Art, June 6, 1916. Bulletin of The Cleveland Museum of Art,
Third Year, July, 1916, pp. 18-19.

90

A Note on the Book of the Locomobile [book designed and executed by T. M. Cleland]. Printing Art, vol. 28, December, 1916,
pp. 277-278.

91

[Remarks on the art museum as related to industry]. Proceedings
of the American Association of Museums, vol. 11, 1917, p. 95.

Report of the Committee on Publications. Grolier Club Year Book, 1917, pp. 120-127.

What the Community Expects [contributions to "The Art Library and the Designer: A Symposium"]. Library Journal, vol. 42, February, 1917, pp. 89-90.

*Articles by
H. W. Kent in
Periodicals and
Newspapers*

94
Report of the Committee on Publications. Grolier Club Year Book, 1918, pp. 52-55.

95
The Metropolitan Museum in Its National Aspects. Bulletin of The Metropolitan Museum of Art, vol. 14, September, 1919, pp. 201-202.

96
Report of the Committee on Publications. Grolier Club Year Book, 1920, pp. 67-72.

97
The Metropolitan Museum of Art. All the Arts: . . . Official Organ of the Detroit Orchestral Association, vol. 3, June, 1920, pp. 12-14.

98
National Style Comes with Rational Taste: Art, Handmade of Old, Will Make the Machine Its Handmaiden When Manufacturers Give the Public What the Public Needs [from an address before the Convention of the American Federation of Arts]. Evening Post, New York, July 17, 1920, Section IV (Saturday Magazine), p. 5.

99
Address of the President. Grolier Club Year Book, 1921, pp. 69-78.

100
Reports of the Trustees for the Years 1920 to 1940. The Metropolitan Museum of Art, . . . Annual Report of the Trustees [for the years 1920-1940]. . . . New York: The Metropolitan Museum of Art, 1921-1941.

The Reports of the Trustees for the Years 1920 to 1931, embracing some thirty or forty pages in the *Annual Reports*, were signed by Henry W. Kent (*or* H. W. Kent), Secretary, and the President (Robert

187

W. de Forest from 1920 to 1930, William Sloane Coffin in 1931). In the *Report* for 1932, the opening six pages are signed "Henry W. Kent, Secretary," and "William Sloane Coffin, President"; the report of the Director is signed by him and those of the Departments by their heads. This practice continues for the balance of the reports. The opening pages of the Report for 1933 are signed by Henry W. Kent, Secretary, and Myron C. Taylor, First Vice-President. From 1934 to 1940, the opening pages are signed "For the Trustees, George Blumenthal, President, H. W. Kent, Secretary."

Articles by W. H. Kent in Periodicals and Newspapers

Mr. Kent undoubtedly also had much to do, editorially, with the statistical tables, etc., included in the *Annual Reports*.

101

Putting Art into Labor: Responsibilities in Our Social System [from an address at the Tenth Annual Convention of the American Federation of Arts]. Good Furniture, vol. 17, September, 1921, pp. 134-136.

102

The Address of the President. Grolier Club Year Book, 1922, pp. 69-77.

103

Our Native Craftsmen. Bulletin of The Metropolitan Museum of Art, vol. 17, November, 1922, part 2 (An American Wing for The Metropolitan Museum of Art: The Gift of Robert W. de Forest and Emily Johnston de Forest), pp. 10-11.

104

The Bolles Collection of American Furniture. *Ibid.*, pp. 12-13.

105

The American Wing in Its Relation to the History of Museum Development. *Ibid.*, pp. 14-16.

106

Address of the President. Grolier Club Year Book, 1923, pp. 73-83.

107

The Glebe-House, Woodbury, Connecticut. Old-Time New England: The Bulletin of the Society for the Preservation of New England Antiquities, vol. 13, April, 1923, pp. 169-173.

108

An Early Printing Press [The Raimondi Press]. Gazette of The Grolier Club, [vol. 1], no. 5, May, 1923, pp. 101-102.

188

109

Museum Labels. Museum Work, vol. 6, July-August, 1923, pp. 55-58.

110
Forty Years: A Retrospect [address read by the President of The Grolier Club at the Fortieth Annual Meeting, held January 24, 1924]. Grolier Club Year Book, 1924, pp. 73-93.

111
The Gift of the Morgan Library. Gazette of The Grolier Club, [vol. 1], no. 6, May, 1924, pp. 117-119.

112
How the Metropolitan Museum of Art Serves as a Laboratory for the So-Called Art Trades, *under* Now My Idea Is This! Daily Talks with Thinking New Yorkers on Subjects They Know Best. New York Evening Post, June 17, 1924, p. 10.

113
An Expression from Mr. Kent [letter concerning the Craftsmen Number of The American Printer, August 5, 1924]. American Printer, vol. 79, September 5, 1924, p. 42.

114
[Tribute to Beverly Chew]. Gazette of The Grolier Club, [vol. 1], no. 7, January, 1925, pp. 135-138.

115
The American Heritage in Art [address delivered at the Seventeenth Annual Convention of the American Federation of Arts, Annapolis, Md., May 13, 1926]. American Magazine of Art, vol. 17, July, 1926, pp. 331-334.

116
Public Interests in Art. Journal of the National Education Association, vol. 16, May, 1927, pp. 151-154.

117
Museums of Art. Architectural Forum, vol. 47, December, 1927, pp. 581-584.

118
A State of Mind. Walpole Society Note Book, 1928, pp. 23-26.

119
The Monument of General Richard Montgomery. Year-Book

and Register of the Parish of Trinity Church, in the City of New York, 1929, pp. 292-306.

120

Modern Art Makes Itself at Home. Woman's Home Companion, vol. 56, January, 1929, pp. 11-12.

121

The Motive of the Exhibition of American Industrial Art. Bulletin of The Metropolitan Museum of Art, vol. 24, April, 1929, pp. 96-97.

122

Its Public Library [letter to the Editor dated May 16, 1929]. Brooklyn Daily Times, May 19, 1929, Section I, p. 4.

123

H. W. Kent Addresses Yale Art Graduates: Says Machine and Department Store Have Changed Public Attitude toward Art [excerpt from Art in the Future, address at the Anniversary Exercises of the Yale School of Fine Arts, June 13, 1929]. Waterbury Democrat, June 14, 1929, p. 5.

The address was widely quoted, in excerpts ranging from a few phrases to several paragraphs. It was apparently never published in its entirety. See also following entry.

124

Machine, Department Store, and the Public Attitude toward Art [excerpt from Art in the Future, address at the Anniversary Exercises of the Yale School of Fine Arts]. Art and Archaeology, vol. 28, September, 1929, p. 97.

See note on preceding entry.

125

Another Day: A Retrospective Note on Thomas Frognall Dibdin and the Printers of the Shakespeare Press. Colophon: A Book Collectors' Quarterly, part 2, May, 1930, [no pagination; article composed of front., 16 pp., and facsimiles tipped in].

126

Van Braam Houckgeest, an Early American Collector. Proceedings of the American Antiquarian Society, n.s. vol. 40, part 2, October, 1930, pp. 159-174.

127

Robert W. de Forest. Bulletin of The Metropolitan Museum of Art, vol. 26, June, 1931, pp. 139-140.

Address by Mr. Kent. Bulletin of The Rhode Island School of Design, vol. 19, July, 1931, part 2 (Exercises in Remembrance of Eliza Greene Radeke, late President of The Rhode Island School of Design), pp. 56-59.

Articles by
H. W. Kent in
Periodicals and
Newspapers

The Why and Wherefore of Museum Planning. Architectural Forum, vol. 56, June, 1932, pp. 529-532.

The Fitzwilliam Museum's New Courtauld Gallery. Museum News, vol. 10, September 15, 1932, pp. 7-8.

An Extract from the Statement of The Walpole Society regarding its Publications, 1913-1933. Walpole Society Note Book, 1933, pp. 17-18.

Kent speaks, *under* In Memoriam: George Shepard Palmer, Yale 1878, March 20, 1855-January 23, 1934, by Norman Morrison Isham. Walpole Society Note Book, 1934, pp. 65-67.

[Letter to the American Federation of Arts on its twenty-fifth anniversary]. American Magazine of Art, vol. 27, September, 1934, part 2 (Anniversary Supplement: Proceedings of the Twenty-fifth Annual Convention of the American Federation of Arts, Washington, D. C., May 14-16, 1934), p. 22.

Salomon's House—Research in Art Museums [paper read at the Annual Meeting of the American Association of Museums, Toronto, May 30-June 1, 1934]. Museum News, vol. 13, June 1, 1935, pp. 7-8.

[Tribute to Miss Ruth Shepard Granniss]. Gazette of The Grolier Club, vol. 2, no. 2, May, 1936, pp. 47-48.

A Message from Mr. Kent. News Letter of The American Institute of Graphic Arts, no. 40, July, 1936, p. 1.

An Appreciation [of Frederic Goudy]. Ulster-Irish Society Year
Book, 1937, pp. 25-26.

138

The Narragansett Country. Walpole Society Note Book, 1937,
pp. 34-38.

139

Reminiscences of Early Days [paper presented at the Fiftieth Anniversary of the Columbia School of Library Service, January 5,
1937]. Library Journal, vol. 62, February 15, 1937, pp. 146-148.

140

The President's Address at the Annual Meeting, May 19. News-
Letter of The American Institute of Graphic Arts, no. 44,
August, 1937, pp. 1, 5.

141

[Excerpt from address given at opening of exhibition, The
Work of W. A. Dwiggins, Gallery of the Architectural League,
November 18, 1937], *under* Two Addresses, Subject: Dwiggins.
News-Letter of The American Institute of Graphic Arts, no. 46,
December, 1937, pp. 4-5.

142

[Introduction to] The Fifty Books of the Year: A Cumulative
List of the Examples of Bookmaking Selected and Shown by The
American Institute of Graphic Arts. The Annual of Bookmaking, [vol. 1], 1938, [no pagination; first article; introduction
covers 2 pp.].
Reprinted as American Institute of Graphic Arts Keepsake No. 59,
[1938].

143

Annual Report of the President, May 19, 1938. News-Letter of
The American Institute of Graphic Arts, no. 49, June, 1938,
Supplement [2 pp.].

144

Annual Report of the President, May 31, 1939. News-Letter of
The American Institute of Graphic Arts, no. 53, July, 1939,
pp. 10-11.

145

[Letter to Mr. M. D. C. Crawford dated September 13, 1940],
under Letters to the Editor: Urges Designers Avail Themselves

of N. Y. Museums' Free Aid, by M. D. C. Crawford. Women's
Wear Daily, September 17, 1940, p. 8.

146

The Animal Kingdom, *under* Notes for Bibliophiles. New York
Herald-Tribune, December 29, 1940, Section IX (Books), p. 14.

147

Henry Wood Erving, 1851-1941: Member of The Walpole Society, 1910-1941. Walpole Society Note Book, 1941, pp. 9-12.

148

To Members of The Walpole Society: A Paper Read at the
Thirty-first Annual Meeting, held in Boston on May 4, 1941.
Ibid., pp. 36-38.

149

Richard Townley Haines Halsey, 1865-1942: A Member of The
Walpole Society from 1914. Walpole Society Note Book, 1942,
pp. 17-25.

150

Concerning the Backus Diary [letter to Morgan Brainard dated
July 31, 1941]. *Ibid.*, pp. 45-49.

151

Printer-Philosopher: A Memory of the Late Daniel Berkeley
Updike [letter dated Dec. 31, 1941]. New York Herald Tribune,
January 2, 1942, p. 14.

152

50 Books of the Year 1942: An Address. Print: A Quarterly
Journal of the Graphic Arts, vol. 3, no. 1, Spring, 1942, pp. 1-6.
Also printed as American Institute of Graphic Arts Keepsake No. 69,
1942.

153

Our "Incunabula." New York Library Club Bulletin, vol. 30,
May, 1942, pp. 13-15.

154

Norman Morrison Isham: In Memoriam. Walpole Society Note
Book, 1943, pp. 14-16.

155

An Address by Henry Watson Kent at the Thirty-third Annual
Meeting. *Ibid.*, pp. 20-22.

Dick Canfield. Walpole Society Note Book, 1944, pp. 32-40.

157

Dwight Blaney: Member of The Walpole Society, 1910-1944. Walpole Society Note Book, 1945, pp. 25-32.

158

Antiquaries. Walpole Society Note Book, 1946, pp. 13-17.

Books, Pamphlets, and Periodicals

Edited by Henry Watson Kent

159

A Catalogue of Etchings, Dry-Points, and Mezzotints by Sir Francis Seymour Haden, F.R.C.S., P.R.E., Exhibited at The Grolier Club, 29 East 32d Street, from April 17 to May 10, 1902. [New York: The Grolier Club, 1902].

160

Librarian, a translation of the article from Etienne Gabriel Peignot's Dictionnaire raisonné de bibliologie, Paris, 1802. Published by John Cotton Dana and Henry W. Kent, 1904.

"Broadside, with initial and border in red," announced in the *Library Journal*, vol. 29, August, 1904, p. 445. I have never seen a copy. See above, p. 119.

161

First Editions of the Works of Nathaniel Hawthorne together with Some Manuscripts, Letters, and Portraits Exhibited at The Grolier Club from December 8 to December 24, 1904. New York: The Grolier Club, 1904.

The earlier list of Mr. Kent's writing said of this publication, "Compiled by J. C. Chamberlain [a Grolier Club member] and H. W. Kent." The catalogue itself and the Grolier Club records give no attribution. The catalogue was mentioned on Mr. Kent's list of Grolier Club publications with which he had to do, but in going over the list, he spoke of himself as editor, not author of it.

162

Bulletin of The Metropolitan Museum of Art, vol. 1, no. 1, November, 1905, through vol. 11, no. 12, December, 1916. A monthly from January, 1906.

The issues of November, 1905, and January, 1906, said: "published under the direction of the Secretary's Office. Communications to be addressed to Henry W. Kent, Assistant Secretary." In February, 1906, this became: "Published under the direction of the Secretary. Communications to be addressed to the editor, Henry W. Kent, Assistant Secretary." This statement continued (except for a change to "Henry W. Kent, Secretary," from November, 1913, on) until January, 1917, when it began to read: "Published monthly under the direction of the Secretary of The Metropolitan Museum of Art." From this time, Miss Winifred E. Howe, the Museum's Editor of Publications, may be considered the Editor of the *Bulletin*, though her name was not listed in the magazine as Editor of Publications until May, 1921, or as Editor of the *Bulletin* until November, 1929. Mr. Kent exercised an over-all supervision of the *Bulletin* until his retirement at the end of 1940.

Books, Pamphlets and Periodicals Edited by H. W. Kent

163

The Duties & Qualifications of a Librarian: A Discourse Pronounced in the General Assembly of the Sorbonne December 23, 1780. By Jean-Baptiste Cotton des Houssayes. Literature of Libraries in the Seventeenth and Eighteenth Centuries, edited by John Cotton Dana and Henry W. Kent, No. 1. Chicago, Ill.: A. C. McClurg & Co., 1906.

See above, pp. 118-119. Bibliographical Note not signed; possibly H. W. K.

164

The Reformed Librarie-Keeper: or Two Copies of Letters concerning the Place and Office of a Librarie-Keeper. By John Dury. Literature of Libraries in the Seventeenth and Eighteenth Centuries, edited by John Cotton Dana and Henry W. Kent, No. 2. Chicago, Ill.: A. C. McClurg & Co., 1906.

See above, pp. 118-119. Biographical Sketch by Ruth Shepard Granniss.

165

The Life of Sir Thomas Bodley Written by Himself, together with the First Draft of the Statutes of the Public Library at Oxon. Literature of Libraries in the Seventeenth and Eighteenth Centuries, edited by John Cotton Dana and Henry W. Kent, No. 3. Chicago, Ill.: A. C. McClurg & Co., 1906.

See above, pp. 118-119. Preface by Ruth Shepard Granniss.

Two Tracts on the Founding and Maintaining of Parochial Libraries in Scotland. By James Kirkwood. Literature of Libraries in the Seventeenth and Eighteenth Centuries, edited by John Cotton Dana and Henry W. Kent, No. 4. Chicago, Ill.: A. C. McClurg & Co., 1906.

See above, pp. 118-119. Note not signed.

Books, Pamphlets and Periodicals Edited by H. W. Kent

167

An Exhibition of Some of the Latest Artistic Bindings Done at The Club Bindery, 114 West 32d Street, New York. New York: The Grolier Club, April 26 - May 12, 1906.

168

A Brief Outline of the History of Libraries. By Justus Lipsius. Translated from the second edition (Antwerp, The Plantin Press, John Moretus, 1607), the last from the hand of the author, by John Cotton Dana. Literature of Libraries in the Seventeenth and Eighteenth Centuries, edited by John Cotton Dana and Henry W. Kent, No. 5. Chicago, Ill.: A. C. McClurg & Co., 1907.

See above, pp. 118-119. Introductory Note signed "H.W.K." Translator's Note signed "J.C.D."

169

News from France, or A Description of the Library of Cardinal Mazarin, Preceded by the Surrender of the Library (Now Newly Translated). Two Tracts Written by Gabriel Naudé. Literature of Libraries in the Seventeenth and Eighteenth Centuries, edited by John Cotton Dana and Henry W. Kent, No. 6. Chicago, Ill.: A. C. McClurg & Co., 1907.

See above, pp. 118-119. Biographical Sketch by Ruth Shepard Granniss.

170

Catalogue of a Memorial Exhibition of the Works of Augustus Saint-Gaudens. New York: The Metropolitan Museum of Art, 1908.

Mr. Kent was Secretary of the Committee on the Exhibition and seems to have supervised closely the making of the catalogue, if he did not actually compile it. In the earlier list of his work.

171

The Old Librarian's Almanack. By Φιλόβιβλος [*i.e.* Jared Bean, *i.e.* Edmund Lester Pearson]. A very rare pamphlet first pub-

196

lished in New Haven Connecticut in 1773 and now reprinted for the first time. The Librarian's Series, edited by John Cotton Dana and Henry W. Kent, No. 1. Woodstock, Vt.: The Elm Tree Press, 1909.

See above, p. 119.
Cover has the date 1774.

172

The Library and the Librarian: A Selection of Articles from the Boston Evening Transcript and Other Sources. By Edmund Lester Pearson. The Librarian's Series, edited by John Cotton Dana and Henry W. Kent, No. 2. Woodstock, Vt.: The Elm Tree Press, 1910.

173

Catalogue of an Exhibition of Silver Used in New York, New Jersey, and the South, with a note on Early New York Silversmiths by R. T. Haines Halsey. New York: The Metropolitan Museum of Art, November 6 to December 31, 1911.

174

The Intellectual Torch: Developing a Plan for the Universal Dissemination of Knowledge and Virtue by Means of Free Public Libraries. By Jesse Torrey, Jun. The Librarian's Series, edited by John Cotton Dana and Henry W. Kent, No. 3. Woodstock, Vt.: The Elm Tree Press, 1912.

175

What The Metropolitan Museum of Art Is Doing. New York: The Metropolitan Museum of Art, 1913, 1914, 1915, 1916, 1918, 1919, 1923, 1925, 1927, 1934, 1938.
Title varies: as above, through 1919; *The Metropolitan Museum of Art & What It Is Doing*, in 1923 and 1925; *The Metropolitan Museum of Art, What It Is & What It Does: A Dictionary of Museum Facts and Activities*, in 1927; *The Metropolitan Museum of Art, A Dictionary of Facts and Activities Showing What the Museum Is and What It Does*, in 1934 and 1938. After 1927 commonly referred to as the *Dictionary*. Preface in 1927 and 1934 signed "H. W. Kent, Secretary." Printed by The Gilliss Press in 1913, The Museum Press in 1914-1925 and 1934, The Merrymount Press in 1927, The Spiral Press in 1938.

176

Essay on Bibliography and on the Attainments of a Librarian. By Parent the Elder. Translated by Mrs. Schuyler Van Rensse-

197

laer. The Librarian's Series, edited by John Cotton Dana and Henry W. Kent, No. 4. Woodstock, Vt.: The Elm Tree Press, 1914.

Introductory Note signed "H.W.K."

177

Publications on Sale. New York: The Metropolitan Museum of Art, 1915, 1916, 1917, 1920, 1922, 1923, 1925, 1928, 1930, 1932, 1934, 1935, 1937, 1938, 1940.

Note on Museum Publications in edition of 1928 signed "H. W. Kent, Secretary." Note in all subsequent editions signed "Henry W. Kent, Secretary."

178

To the Committee on Educational Work [report of educational work of the Museum for the year 1915]. [New York]: The Metropolitan Museum of Art, [1916].

Pages 1-2 signed "Henry W. Kent, Secretary" and dated January 14, 1916; followed by separate reports individually signed.

179

The Training of the Librarian. By Friedrich Adolph Ebert. Translated from the second, 1820, German Edition. The Librarian's Series, edited by John Cotton Dana and Henry W. Kent, No. 5. Woodstock, Vt.: The Elm Tree Press, 1916.

Various other volumes were announced at different times for The Librarian's Series: *The Rev. John Sharpe and his Proposal for a Publick Library at New York, 1713,* by Austin Baxter Keep; *Some of the Best Books on the History and Administration of Libraries Published Prior to 1800,* compiled by Beatrice Winser; *The Hoax Concerning the Burning of the Alexandrian Library,* by Joseph Octave Delepierre, London, 1860-61, translated and annotated by George Parker Winship; *The Early History of Libraries,* by Karl Dziatzko, the article in Pauly's *Encyclopaedia of Classical Antiquities,* translated and adapted by Edward Harmon Virgin; *Justin Winsor as a Librarian,* by George Parker Winship. None of these seem to have been published.

180

To the Committee on Educational Work [report of educational work of the Museum for the year 1917]. [New York]: The Metropolitan Museum of Art, n.d.

Signed at the end "Henry W. Kent, Secretary"; largely composed of extracts from five reports of individual staff members.

181

Reproductions on Sale. New York: The Metropolitan Museum of Art, 1920, 1921, 1922, 1924, 1926, 1927, 1929, 1930, 1933.

Title varies: *Photographs, Half-Tones, and Postcards on Sale*, in 1920; *Reproductions; Reproductions on Sale;* in 1927, 1929, and 1930, *Reproductions on Sale of Objects in the Collection: A Cyclopedia of Information.* A part of the material was published in 1928 as *Photographs of Paintings on Sale.* In 1933, *A Cyclopedia of Reproductions on Sale* was issued in four separate parts. There were subsequent editions of Part I in 1936 and 1939; of Part II in 1939; of Part III in 1937 and 1940; and of Part IV in 1936. The opening note, variously titled, was usually signed "Henry W. Kent [or "H. W. Kent"], Secretary." Editions of 1927 and 1930 were printed by The Merrymount Press.

Books, Pamphlets and Periodicals Edited by H. W. Kent

182

The Fiftieth Anniversary Celebration, MDCCCLXX-MCMXX. New York: The Metropolitan Museum of Art, 1921.

183

A Review of Fifty Years' Development Printed on the Occasion of the Fiftieth Anniversary of the Founding of the Museum. New York: The Metropolitan Museum of Art, [1921].

184

Christmas Gifts: Suggestions and Hints. New York: The Metropolitan Museum of Art, 1921-1923, 1925-1940.

Title varies: *Christmas Suggestions, Suggestions for Christmas Gifts,* etc. Usually signed at the end "H. W. Kent [or "Henry W. Kent"], Secretary." No copy has been found for 1924, but a folder may have been printed.

185

An Almanac for the year 1930, being the Sixtieth in the History of The Metropolitan Museum of Art. New York: The Metropolitan Museum of Art, 1930.

Printed at The Museum Press For the Members of the Corporation.

INDEX

Abbot, Edith R., 64-65
Adams, Edward D., 98
American Antiquarian Society, 80
American architecture. See under Architecture
American Association of Museums, xi, xii, 97, 142, 150-151, 156, 165, 167
American decorative arts: in Norwichtown, xi, 7-8, 59, 75, 78-79, 80-81, 83, 84, 160; in Hudson-Fulton exhibition, xi, 83-84, 160, 163, 164; collectors of, xii, 80-81, 84, 127, 160, 161-162; Norton on, 47-48, 84; Gilman on, 51-52, 84; public and museum attitude toward, 84, 109, 162-163, 164; purchase of Bolles collection for Metropolitan Museum, 160-161. See also Industrial Art
American Federation of Arts, 60, 97, 165, 167
American Institute of Graphic Arts, 131-133, 152, 172-173
American Library Association, 14-15, 16, 72, 102
American Wing. See under Metropolitan Museum of Art, Departments and divisions
Americana. See American decorative arts
Andrews, William Loring, 59, 98, 114, 115, 117, 121-122, 123, 126
Annmary Brown Memorial, 124
Appleton, Sumner, 160
Architecture
    American: lectures and book on, by Fiske Kimball, xii; in Norwichtown, 2, 4, 8, 81, 83, 84; Columbia College Library, 11; Ware's influence on, 17-18; Norton on, 46, 47-48, 84; and American Wing, 164
    Byzantine, 87, 88-89
    Greek, See Greek art and archaeology
    Of museums, 91-92, 163-165
    Reproductions (casts and photographs) and books, 20, 41, 97, 101, 106, 108
Arms, Hiram P., D.D., 4, 6
Arnold, Benedict, 79-80
Art, history of: 19th cent. books on, 19; and museum administration, 19, 138, 165-166; teaching of, 45, 55, 66, 107, 146-149; students of, as museum visitors, 144, 149, 158, 167

Art Congress for the Development of Drawing and Art Teaching, 145-146
Art-in-Trades Club, 155-156, 157
Art Students' League, 66, 67-68
Arts and crafts, American. See American decorative arts; Industrial art
Arts and Crafts Societies, 154
Arts of the book. See Book arts
Athens, H. W. K. in, 87-88, 89-90, 92
Atterbury, Grosvenor, 164
Avery, Samuel P., 20, 59, 98, 114, 115, 117, 121, 122-123

Bach, Richard F., 156-157
Backus family, 76, 82-83
Baker, George F., 98, 140
Baker, George Hall, 12
Baker, William G., 12
Barbizon School, paintings, 31, 57-58, 122
Barnard, Frederick A. P., 11, 16
Barnard College, founding of, 20
Bayle, Pierre, Dictionary, 129
Beaman, C. C., 98
Bean, Jared, 119
Benedick, The, apartment house, 139
Benson, E. F., 88
Berenson, Bernhard, 68
Berenson, Mrs. Bernhard, 146
Berlin, museums, 91, 92, 97
Bibliography, 16, 17, 69, 116-117, 118, 120, 121, 123, 126, 128, 131
Bibliophiles and bibliophily, 3, 14, 15, 115, 116, 122, 123, 127, 128. See also Book arts and its cross references; Book collectors
Billings, Dr. John Shaw, 127, 129
Biscoe, Walter Stanley, 12, 14
Blake, William, 121, 124
Blaney, Dwight, 81, 84, 161
Bode, Wilhelm, xi, 91, 155
Bolles, Eugene, and Bolles collection, 80-81, 84, 160-161
Book arts, 113-114, 116-118, 120, 129, 132. See also Bookbinding; Printing and typographical design; Prints and book illustration
Book collectors, 14, 114, 116, 124, 162
Bookbinding, 69, 70, 116; Dewey's attitude toward, 13, 14; Phoenix collection, Columbia Library, 19; exhibition in Slater Museum, 59; and Grolier Club,

204

London, 115, 117, 121, 146, 154-155. *See also* South Kensington Museum
Loring, Charles G., 43-44
Louvre, 92, 143
Lowell lectures, 148
Lydenberg, Harry Miller, 127
Lythgoe, Albert, 88

McKim, Mead & White, 139, 164
Mansfield, Howard, 98, 115
Mansfield, Richard, 130
Marquand, Henry G., and Marquand collection, 97, 100-101
Mason, Major John, 76
Mather, Frank Jewett, 148
Matthews, Brander, 116, 134 n.
Mechlin, Leila, 165
Melcher, Frederic G., citation by, 132-133
Merriam, A. C., 98
Metric system, 13, 16
Metropolitan Museum of Art: *History*, by W. E. Howe, vi, xii-xiii; administration, xi, 135-136, 141-143, 150, 172; Trustees, 18, 97-100, 137, 141, 142, 145, 147, 164; museum furniture, 92, 93, 170; cast collections, 97-101, 105, 108; early years, 135-138, 147, 150, 153; Charter, 137, 145, 147, 153, 155, 159
Departments and divisions: Library and reference collection of photographs, xi, 149; educational work, xi, xii, 143-150, 157-158, 171; industrial art, xi, 133, 144, 145, 147, 153-160; American Wing, xi, xii, 7, 81, 84, 127, 161, 162-164; Dept of Paintings, 68, 130; Information Desk, 68, 72, 142, 153; Dept of Prints, 127; Catalogue Division, 142-143; Photographic Studio, 143, 148. *See also below under* Printing and publications
Printing and publications, 153, 169-171, 173; Editor of Publications and Editorial Division, 72, 150, 152, 170, 173; H. W. K. as director of publications, 126, 133, 149-151, 170-171; Museum Press, 133, 150-152, 171; *Bulletin*, 150, 172; exhibition of Museum's printing, 151-152
See also Hudson-Fulton exhibition
Meyer, Annie Nathan (Mrs. Alfred), 20
Miantonomo, Narragansett chief, 77-78
Milla, Edward, 143
Miller, Charles R., 129
Millet, F. D., 98
Mitchell, Donald G. ("Ik Marvel"), 70

Monreale, 87
Morgan, J. Pierpont, 137, 141
Morgan Library. *See* Pierpont Morgan Library
Morris, William, 115, 125, 126, 154-155, 159
Morse, Professor, talks on Japanese art, 69
Morse, Kate, 67, 70
Morton, Joseph L., 114
Motion pictures, 149, 158
Mount Holyoke Seminary, 107
Munich, museums of, 91, 92, 155
Musée Galliéra, Paris, 91, 92
Museum of Fine Arts, Boston, 18, 39, 43, 44, 56, 58, 71, 97, 162, 163, 166; art school, 66, 67
Museum Press. *See under* Metropolitan Museum of Art, Printing and publications
Museums: training for work in, vi, 9, 17, 18, 83, 127, 135, 138, 165-166; European, H. W. K.'s study of, xi, 89-93, 139, 155; and education, xi, 17, 49-50, 96, 101, 103-104, 110, 144, 146, 167; and industrial art, xi, 47-48, 51-52, 84, 96, 155, 158-160; methods of display, xi, 90-91, 143, 157; administration, xi, 19, 90-91, 92-93, 165; public relations, 17, 90, 102, 143, 153, *see also above* and education *and* and industrial art; need of young men, 18, 21, 135; acquisition of objects of art, 19, 109-110, 157, 162, 167; Boards of Trustees, 19, 103, 141; intermuseum association, 60, 73, 165; visitors to, individuals and types, 60-62, 104, 144-145, 167; printing, 90, 133; furniture for, 90, 92-93, 102-103, 104, 105; architecture of, 91-92, 163-165; offices, 136, 165. *See also* American Association of Museums; American decorative arts, public and museum attitude toward; Casts; Labels and label holders; Metropolitan Museum of Art; Museum of Fine Arts; Photographs; Slater Memorial Museum

National Academy of Design, 56
New York, 108, 166; H. W. K.'s living quarters in, 20-21, 139; guests from, at Slater Museum opening, 42; character of, in 1900, 114; books and prints on, 121-122, 126; R. W. de Forest's contribution to, 140. *See also* Columbia College and University; Grolier Club; Metropolitan Museum of Art
New York Central Railroad, 11, 20
New York Library Club, 128

Robinson, Edward, 18, 45, 58, 87, 90; and Slater Museum, 39-42, 44, 50, 56-57, 61, 96, 99, 111 n.; and Metropolitan Museum, 97-98, 100, 137, 138, 162; and Springfield museum, 102, 105
Robinson, Juliet, W., 68, 72, 153
Rogers, Bruce, 118, 125, 126, 129-130, 133, 151, 152
Rollins, Carl P., 125, 133, 152
Root, Elihu, 141, 165, 166
Ruskin, John, 3, 50, 154, 159
Ruzicka, Rudolph, 126, 152

Sage, Mrs. Russell, 161
Saint-Gaudens, Augustus, 98
School Art League, 147
School of Library Economy. See under Columbia College and University
Shipman, Father, 4
Shipman, N. L., Esq., 78
Sigourney, Lydia Huntley, 2
Simplified spelling, 13, 16
Slater, John, 30
Slater, John Fox, 29, 30
Slater, Samuel, 30
Slater, William A., 23, 42, 45, 64, 87, 98; gift of Slater Memorial building, 28-29, 31; gift of Slater Memorial Museum, 32, 39, 43, 105; objects from his collections, exhibitions and catalogues, 57-58, 59, 66; encourages museums of reproductions, 95, 96, 104
Slater Memorial building, 28-29, 35, 41; dedication, 29-30, 32-34, 36 n., 95; use of lecture hall and classrooms, 32-33, 35-36, 68-69. See also Slater Memorial Museum
Slater Memorial Museum, v-vi, xii, 92-93; foundation, 23-24, 31-34, 39; relation to Norwich Free Academy, 23, 62; reputation and influence, 23, 39, 41, 42, 61, 102, 106, 107-108, 110; contents and installation, 39-42, 100; opening, 42-53, 84; use by Academy students, 55-56; use by Art School students, 56, 58, 62, 65, 66; attendance, 56-57, 61-62; exhibitions, 57-61, 68; special exhibition catalogues, 58, 59, 68, 69, 70, 169-170, 172; work with elementary school students, 62-64; catalogue of casts, 69; objects from Norwich exhibited in, 71, 77, 80; cost, 96; visitors from Metropolitan Museum, 98-100
Smith, Charles Stuart, 98
Smith, Francis Hopkinson, 129

Smith, Horace, collection, 102-105
Smith, James M., 101
Society for the Protection of Ancient Buildings, 154-155
South Kensington (Victoria and Albert) Museum, London, 33, 91, 92, 93, 95, 137, 138, 153, 155
Spalding, Philip L., 71
Spenceley, Joseph Winfred, 118
Spencer Collection, N. Y. P. L., 127-128
Springfield, Mass., City Library Association, 60, 82, 92, 101-105, 172
Stedman, Edmund Clarence, 5-6, 75, 79, 128
Stereopticon, 55, 148-149
Stokes, I. N. Phelps, 122, 126
Street, Augustus Russell, 35
Sturgis, Russell, 19, 39, 58
Sudeley, Charles Douglas Richard, 4th baron, 146
Swiss museums, 91, 92, 155, 163

Terwilliger, William James, 12
Textiles and textile manufacture, xii, 30, 58, 65, 91, 92, 155
Thackeray, William Makepeace, 131
Thompson, F. F., 98
Tracy, Calvin, Academy of, 49
Tracy, Dr. Elisha, 77
Trumbull, John, paintings, 59 ,
Trumbull, Jonathan, 7, 79
Tufts, Edith Souther, 103
Twachtman, John H., 43, 67-68
Tyler, Charles H., 160, 161, 163
Typography. See Printing and typographical design
Typothetae, 123

Uncas, Mohegan chief, 77, 78
Uncas, Samuel, Sachem, 77
Updike, Daniel Berkeley, 118, 125, 126, 131, 133, 152

Vatican, 92, 143
Vedder, Mrs. Elihu, 100
Victoria and Albert Museum. See South Kensington Museum
Virgin, Edward H., 119

Walker, Francis A., 43
Walpole, Horace, 4th Earl of Orford, 162
Walpole Society, xii, 161-162, 164
Warde, Frederic, 125
Ware, William R., 17-18, 21, 43, 98, 135
Washington, George, 7
Washington Irving High School, 147
Watson ancestors of H. W. K., 1

207

208

The Committee on Publications of The Grolier

Club certifies that this is one of an edition of

one thousand and twenty-five copies printed in

February 1949 *at The Spiral Press, New York*